DNA MORMON

D. Michael Quinn

DNA MOR MON

Perspectives on the Legacy of Historian **D. Michael Quinn**

edited by

BENJAMIN E. PARK

SIGNATURE BOOKS | 2022 | SALT LAKE CITY

Design by Jason Francis

www.signaturebooks.com

FIRST EDITION | 2022

LIBRARY OF CONGRESS CONTROL NUMBER: 2022947942

Paperback ISBN: 978-1-56085-463-0
Ebook ISBN: 978-1-56085-480-7

CONTENTS

The First Attempts at Examining a Monumental Legacy

BENJAMIN E. PARK

Dennis Michael Quinn had only been working for Leonard Arrington's History Division at the Church of Jesus Christ of Latter-day Saints for a few months before he had become a thorn in the side of archivists. Currently a master's student at the University of Utah in the summer of 1972, Quinn possessed a thin frame, dark long hair, and an insatiable appetite for historical sources. His bloodhound-like knack for finding gems among books, journals, letters, and other documents that had been long sequestered had endeared him to Arrington, the first academic to be appointed the official LDS Church Historian. Quinn would be assigned a task on Monday and would produce a detailed, footnote-rich report that spanned dozens of pages by Friday. However, some of the men who worked in the archives and did not share the new spirit of openness came to see him as a nuisance who disturbed the slumbering past with his frequent requests. They wished he would just leave the past alone.[1]

One archivist, Lauritz Peterson, reached a breaking point when, in late July 1972, Quinn requested the minute books for various Church-related colleges that had not yet been catalogued. Exhausted, Peterson told him to go find the documents himself. "Maybe over there," he directed, pointing to a dimly lit corner of the basement. What Quinn found was breathtaking. "Covered in dust, stacked against the walls and in tall piles across the floor," he later narrated, "were hundreds—perhaps *thousands*—of leather-bound volumes in various sizes." They included Brigham Young's financial records,

---

1. Gary Topping, *D. Michael Quinn: Mormon Historian* (Salt Lake City: Signature Books, 2022), 29.

journals from prominent leaders, First Presidency minutes, and other material that had likely been hidden away since the anti-polygamy raids of the 1880s. Quinn spent the next few hours "sampling this candy-store of Mormon historical documents" without a break. By the time he pried himself away late in the evening and left the basement, he surprised the remaining guards who assumed the entire building was empty.[2]

The moment, though brief, embodied much of the period. The era of "New Mormon History," a movement to understand Mormonism in academic terms, promised a new dawn for the faith. After nearly a century and a half of seeing the past as a battle ground between pro- and anti-Mormon forces, this new generation rooted both in their faith as well as secular academic disciplines attempted to prove that you could pledge allegiance to both. D. Michael Quinn's scholarly work would soon become synonymous with this crusade. After working with Arrington for a few years and completing his master's degree, he moved on to Yale for a PhD, upon the completion of which he was hired to teach history at Brigham Young University. By that point, he had a wife and growing family that, at least outwardly, fulfilled the expectations for the ideal Mormon life. For a while, it seemed the bright future exemplified by those archival discoveries was coming to fruition.

Zion would soon flee. Publicly, Quinn's work clashed against the more devotional and hagiographic standards set by an increasingly antagonistic church leadership. Privately, he struggled to reconcile his long-suppressed homosexuality with the faith's heteronormative expectations. Everything fell apart quickly. By the end of the 1980s, he was divorced, forced to resign from BYU, and lacked stable employment. Then, in September 1993, ecclesiastical leaders excommunicated him from the church, a severing that culminated two tumultuous decades. Quinn was no longer even a member of the church he still believed to be divine. He remained a self-described wanderer until his unexpected death in 2021. Until his last day,

---

2. D. Michael Quinn, *A Chosen Path: A Memoir* (Salt Lake City: Signature Books, forthcoming). Gary James Bergera, ed., *Confessions of a Mormon Historian: The Diaries of Leonard J. Arrington, 1971–1997* (Salt Lake City: Smith-Pettit, 2018), 206 (July 28, 1872).

Quinn insisted that he was a "DNA Mormon"—that his religious connection was blood-deep.

Despite institutional erasure, Quinn's scholarship proved both formidable and lasting. His many books on the Mormon hierarchy, the early faith's involvement with magic culture, and convoluted beliefs and practices concerning sexuality became immediate classics in the field and remain immensely influential today; his many articles on power and violence, visionary experiences, and, especially, post-manifesto polygamous marriages were as monumental and influential as most monographs. Besides being known for his page-long endnotes—"I've become a parody of myself," he once quipped[3]—Quinn's scholarship was consistently bold, brave, and controversial. Much of the modern Mormon studies field is built upon his shoulders.

Yet if Mormons and scholars alike are familiar with his academic work, it is Quinn's personal experiences and beliefs that require more attention. His life exemplified tensions between faith and intellect, obedience and dissent, as well as cultural fissures concerning race and gender. The fact that he, a historian himself, also left a prodigious collection of personal papers makes him a prominent candidate for scholarly engagement. There are few figures through whom the story of modern Mormonism can be told more compellingly than D. Michael Quinn.

This volume attempts to be one of the first scholarly engagements with Quinn's life, times, and legacies. These chapters were originally presented at a conference held at the University of Utah in March 2022. The number of organizations who helped sponsor the event demonstrate Quinn's beloved status: schools like Claremont Graduate University, University of Utah, and Utah State University, as well as non-profit organizations like the Dialogue Foundation, Mormon History Association, the Smith-Pettit Foundation, and the Sunstone Foundation donated money and resources. Barbara Jones Brown, the new executive director of Signature Books, immediately saw the potential for gathering these papers together into

---

3. Lavina Fielding Anderson, "DNA Mormon: D. Michael Quinn," in John Sillito and Susan Saker, eds., *Mormon Mavericks: Essays on Dissenters* (Salt Lake City: Signature Books, 2002), 360.

one volume. All these people and institutions deserve thanks for making this project possible.

This volume is divided into several sections to reflect the goals and purposes of each paper. Neil J. Young's featured essay provides a bird's eye view of Quinn's life and legacy, situating him within several significant historical currents during the second half of the twentieth century. The following section then builds on this foundation by looking at Quinn as a *historical* figure: Gary James Bergera details how Quinn fit into the New Mormon History movement; Sara Patterson examines how Quinn has often been pigeon-holed into heteronormative narratives; Sujey Vega explores how Quinn's father, whose birth name was Daniel Peña, tried to escape his Chicano heritage—and how Quinn himself could never reconcile his identity to this lost past; and finally, Maxine Hanks reflects on Quinn's position as a dissenter within a faith's constantly evolving boundaries. Together, these papers point to how useful the famed historian is when placed within history himself.

The volume then moves to examine Quinn's *historiographical* contributions. Each of the four chapters in this next section focus on a particular topic that was central to his work: Patrick Mason and Hovan Lawton demonstrate the surprisingly "conservative" elements of Quinn's work on the Mormon hierarchy, and why they were present in the first place; Ian Barber dissects the field of folklore and magic, and how Quinn's famous book both fit into and diverged from broader disciplinary discussions; Cristina Rosetti outlines how Quinn's influential article on post-manifesto polygamy launched a new area of study that still deserves attention; and finally, K. Mohrman situates Quinn's work on same-sex attraction within the wider scholarly community that has continued to subvert traditional understandings of gender and sexuality. These essays demonstrate how Quinn's work remains influential, even as scholars have moved beyond his findings and qualified his arguments.

Just as Quinn always cherished the mentorship he received from Leonard Arrington, Quinn himself was known for his support of young scholars. (He was even voted a favorite professor by graduating students shortly before his resignation from BYU.) Therefore, it is only appropriate to feature the works of young scholars who are building on Quinn's scholarly legacy. The third section of papers are written by undergraduate and graduate students working on topics close to Quinn's own corpus: Millie Tullis looks at how a particular folkloric story that involved seer stones and polygamy evolved over the twentieth century; Calvin Burke displays how the institutional problems faced by Eugene England, similar to those faced by Quinn, exemplified broader Mormon cultural fissures; and Brianna Bratsman explores how the most recent debates over sexuality at BYU highlight paradoxes in the modern faith. These authors demonstrate the field's future directions and prove that Quinn has left a solid foundation upon which to build.

The volume concludes with a poignant postscript from Martha Bradley-Evans, a famed historian in her own right who was a contemporary and friend of Quinn's. Scholars today owe a debt of gratitude to their generation for providing the tools, demonstrating the bravery, and pointing the way for the world of Mormonism in general, and Mormon studies in particular.

The Mormon tradition may never have another D. Michael Quinn, but it will have numerous voices who have learned from him and will work to carry on his legacy. This volume is merely one of the first attempts to explore what that legacy meant, both in historical and historiographical terms. As Arrington mused on the eve of Quinn's excommunication in 1993, "historians always have the last word." Quinn would have undoubtedly agreed.[4]

---

4. Bergera, *Confessions*, 617 (Sep. 25, 1993).

A New Mormon History of D. Michael Quinn

NEIL J. YOUNG

A day after his death at the age of 77 in April 2021, D. Michael Quinn had his exceptional life remembered in the pages of the *Salt Lake Tribune*. Written by the *Tribune*'s famed religion reporter, Peggy Fletcher Stack, Quinn's obituary described his upbringing as having taken place "in a Mormon cocoon" and observed that his life of prodigious scholarship on LDS history "put him on a collision course with his church."[1]

Undoubtedly, the Mormon tradition in general, and the Church of Jesus Christ of Latter-day Saints in particular, will stand at the center of any consideration of Quinn's life and legacy. For one who was raised in the Mormon faith, devoted his life to studying and sharing Mormon history, and endured the social and professional price of being excommunicated from the LDS Church, Quinn was inseparable from Mormonism. Yet accounts of his life and scholarship have often seemed caught in their own Mormon cocoons, every moment sketched within and made sense of by the limits of Zion. Given Quinn's role in the development of New Mormon History, and especially his commitment to historical revisionism and humanistic approaches to the past, however, the best way to honor his life and his work may come by repositioning its narrative as an American story rather than a Mormon one.

Such a method not only esteems his life but also allows the fullest understanding of its significance. As Quinn contended, among the strengths of New Mormon History was its attention to "context and

---

1. Peggy Fletcher Stack, "Historian D. Michael Quinn, Who Was Booted from the LDS Church as Part of the 'September Six' But Remained a Believer, Dies at 77," *Salt Lake Tribune*, Apr. 22, 2021, sltrib.com.

details."[2] Yet as his reviewers sometimes responded, Quinn's work often presented an overwhelming abundance of historical details while insufficiently accounting for historical context.[3]

With all that in mind, this essay seeks to invert the typical Quinn quota of details to context by drawing upon selected moments of his biography in order to situate his life and scholarship in the broadest contexts of twentieth-century U.S. history. In thinking about Quinn within the wide contours of modern America, it argues that we can find the largest meanings of his life, his scholarship, and his Mormonism by considering them in the realms of American political, cultural, and religious history, and especially in the field of LGBTQ history. Rather than producing a "Great Man" view of Quinn, something that he would have rejected out of his own sense of history and personal humility, it presents Quinn as an important person who did very good, if imperfect, things, especially for Mormon history and historiography.

Dennis Michael Quinn was born March 26, 1944, in Pasadena, California. In his recent biography of Quinn, Gary Topping used the phrase "ambiguous identities" to talk about the different aspects of Quinn's early life and development.[4] Quinn himself described having a "split identity."[5] Such characterizations reflect the different influences that were at play in his childhood home—and how they were often a source of confusion and conflict for Quinn as he grew up.

Quinn's father, Daniel Peña, was a Chicano-American man, born in Arizona to Mexican immigrants and reared in the Spanish-speaking neighborhoods of East Los Angeles. Shameful of his Mexican identity, Peña tried to cover it up as much as he could. One

2. D. Michael Quinn, "Editor's Introduction," in D. Michael Quinn, ed., *The New Mormon History: Revisionist Essays on the Past* (Salt Lake City: Signature Books, 1992), viii.

3. Benjamin Park, "D. Michael Quinn, Mormon Capitalism, and New Mormon History," *Professor Park's Blog*, Nov. 22, 2017, benjaminepark.com. On the call for New Mormon History to engage deeper contextualization, see Matthew Bowman, "Context and the New-New Mormon History," *Journal of Mormon History* 35, no. 3 (Summer 2009): 208–13.

4. Gary Topping, *D. Michael Quinn: Mormon Historian* (Salt Lake City: Signature Books, 2022), 1.

5. D. Michael Quinn, "On Being a Mormon Historian (and Its Aftermath)," in *Faithful History: Essays on Writing Mormon History*, ed. George D. Smith (Salt Lake City: Signature Books, 1992), 72.

act of subterfuge involved changing his name from "Daniel Peña" to "Donald Quinn," a switch inspired by his childhood friend, Anthony Quinn, who would go on to star in American film classics like *Lawrence of Arabia* and *Lust for Life*. From his father, D. Michael Quinn seemed to learn the slipperiness of identity—that it is not as rigid or fixed as often thought to be, but something that can be chosen and reformulated. And that it can morph over the course of one's life.

Quinn's mother, Joyce Workman, was a redheaded woman of Irish descent. She was also a sixth-generation Mormon. Quinn's father was nominally Catholic and not particularly devout. But the father's large, extended Catholic family compared to Quinn's mother's smaller Mormon family meant that Quinn would describe his early life as taking place in a largely Catholic environment.[6]

The marriage did not last long, ending in divorce around the time that young Quinn was five years old. Even still, the aspects of his parents' background, marriage, and dissolution are useful for considering in the context of post-World War II America and the decade of the 1950s. They also help frame how we understand Quinn as a product of this defining era, especially given how his family and childhood both fit within and stood apart from some of the major historical developments of this period. Quinn came of age during one of the more recognizable eras of American history—a period often more romanticized than accurately portrayed—but a period generally thought of as one of post-war domestic tranquility, material abundance, suburbanization, and cultural conformity.

If these were the themes of this era, they were not necessarily those of Quinn's young life. Indeed, rather than neatly fitting within the safe confines of mid-century America as has been popularly imagined, Quinn's family and childhood instead exemplified the period's untidier historical currents, such as those that the historian Stephanie Coontz has written about. Coontz showed in her 1992 work *The Way We Never Were* that the era's "Leave It To Beaver" depiction of familial bliss was not the norm but a new creation that misrepresented how many American families were made up of two working parents and struggled with significant challenges, including

---

6. Quinn biographical details from Topping, *D. Michael Quinn*, 1–6.

high rates of poverty, domestic violence, and substance abuse.[7] Tracing the various points of convergence and divergence between the actual circumstances of Quinn's developmental years and 1950s America's hegemonic culture and politics illuminates how the pressures and expectations of this period would have shaped someone like Quinn and other Americans who didn't neatly embody or fulfill so many of its cultural messages, images, and representations.

One critically important way in which Quinn's early life did align more closely with the spirit of the era, however, was with regard to religion and his religious faith. Growing up in the 1950s, Quinn lived in a period of heightened religiosity that was in turn shaped and exacerbated by the era's anti-communist politics and the national project to define the United States in opposition to the Soviet Union's "Godless communism." In this political environment, church attendance and membership skyrocketed. In 1930, only 47 percent of Americans had belonged to churches; by 1960 nearly 70 percent did. While Americans were filling up church pews, the federal government made notable changes, like adding "under God" to the Pledge of Allegiance and "In God we trust" to the nation's currency.[8] Seen from this perspective, Quinn's or any other Mormon's religious faith and devotion at the time was hardly "peculiar," but rather paradigmatic.

Yet critics at the time and scholars hence characterized many of these acts as more performative than sincere, additional evidence of the era's social pressures of conformity and conservatism. As president-elect in 1952, Dwight D. Eisenhower unwittingly voiced how the period's religiosity contained its own ambivalence. "Our form of government has no sense unless it is founded in a deeply religious faith," Eisenhower said, "and I don't care what it is."[9] Such indifference suggested, as many religious leaders then worried, that mid-century America placed more importance on religion as a form

---

7. Stephanie Coontz, *The Way We Never Were: American Families and the Nostalgia Trap* (New York: Basic Books, 1992).

8. Neil J. Young, *We Gather Together: The Religious Right and the Problem of Interfaith Politics* (New York: Oxford University Press, 2016), 9. See also, Kevin M. Kruse, *One Nation Under God: How Corporate America Invented Christian America* (New York: Basic Books, 2015).

9. Young, *We Gather Together*, 9.

of public identity than as a personal faith, but that cultural anxiety may have sharpened Quinn's focus on the sincerity of belief he would show throughout his scholarship.

That same year, the eight-year-old D. Michael Quinn was baptized into the Church of Jesus Christ of Latter-day Saints. Quinn's decision to do so had been deeply shaped by the devout and sometimes overbearing example of his grandmother, his chief caregiver in the years after his parents' divorce.[10] But before that, the fact that Quinn was raised in an interreligious family would have been rare at the time. Indeed, the U.S. rates of interfaith marriage remained incredibly low until the 1960s and didn't accelerate until after the 1980s. When Quinn's parents married in the 1940s, interreligious marriages were not only uncommon, but in many ways actively discouraged by denominational leaders and by the U.S. government. Religious authorities spoke out against these marriages mostly for theological reasons, arguing that one's faith would be compromised or even eradicated by coupling with someone from another religious tradition. They warned that children raised in such households would be religiously confused and more likely to develop no faith at all.

The U.S. government emphasized other concerns. During World War II, U.S. Armed Forces published and distributed pamphlets to service members that actively discouraged interfaith marriages. These mixed-religion pairings, the documents warned, were inherently dangerous because they were fundamentally incompatible, and that made them a threat to national strength because they were more prone to fall apart.[11]

Given all this, Quinn's parents' marriage and its dissolution—for whatever reasons it happened—surely spoke to the period's tensions over religious diversity, especially within the American family. In this context, Topping's description of Quinn as having been used as a "pawn" in a religious tug-of-war battle can be understood as rooted in the particular dynamics of his family. It also demonstrates some of the era's very anxieties that viewed any deviance from the

---

10. Topping, *D. Michael Quinn*, 4–5.
11. Samira K. Mehta, *Beyond Chrismukkah: The Christian-Jewish Interfaith Family in the United States* (Chapel Hill: The University of North Carolina Press, 2018), 31–32.

imagined norm of the white, heterosexual, male-breadwinner family as a threat to the nation's security and vitality.[12]

At the same time, these years gave rise to the idea of "Tri-faith America," a growing national appreciation for pluralism and religious tolerance. Will Herberg's 1955 book, *Protestant, Catholic, Jew*, gave the most famous expression of the conception, but religious leaders, academic scholars, and public officials all encouraged widespread acceptance that the American nation was moving from its Protestant past—or, more accurately from a conception of itself as a Protestant nation—to one that recognized religious diversity as a strength of the nation. Such a notion may seem like a contradiction to the era's disapproval of interreligious marriages, but it demonstrates how competing ideals exist in moments where significant historical changes occur. Additionally, the mid-century coexistence of religious fears and ecumenical values made sense given that those decades' overall cultural message was pro-religion.[13]

Mormonism stood rather awkwardly in this tri-faith formulation, in large part because it tended to be placed under the Protestant umbrella. This placement owed mostly to the fact that Mormonism at mid-century wasn't large enough to warrant its own designation in this cultural-religious framework, but also since religion scholars located Mormonism's origins within the long history of Protestant schisms. Yet for their own theological reasons, Protestant and LDS leaders alike objected to Mormonism being named a Protestant sect. Still, its inclusion within the tri-faith model signaled a visibility and respectability LDS officials had aspired to for decades.[14]

In addition to this cultural recognition, the LDS Church enjoyed enormous growth during this period. The faith's explosive expansion surely shaped Quinn's religious development and may have also influenced his lifelong interest in the institution of the church itself. The institutional context is therefore critical. One year before Quinn was baptized, David O. McKay became church president in 1951.

12. Topping, *D. Michael Quinn*, 3.
13. Kevin M. Schultz, *Tri-Faith America: How Catholics and Jews Held Postwar America to Its Protestant Promise* (New York: Oxford University Press, 2011); Will Herberg, *Protestant, Catholic, Jew: An Essay in American Religious Sociology* (Garden City, NY: Doubleday, 1955).
14. Young, *We Gather Together*, 10.

McKay oversaw Mormonism's transformation of the LDS faith from a regional sect into an international religion, accomplished through extensive missionizing and an increase in temple building. McKay's two decades as president showed the fruits of that labor. At his death in 1970, the LDS Church counted 3 million members, up from the 1.1 million Saints when he began.[15] The Los Angeles Temple, Quinn's home city, opened in 1956, making it the tenth dedicated temple and, at the time, the largest. If Southern California Saints had once felt they lived on the periphery of a Mormonism centered around the Intermountain West, the building of the L.A. Temple and the emergence of a global LDS Church in the 1950s and 1960s worked to redraw the map of Mormonism during Quinn's formative years.

The young Quinn's interest in his church grew alongside the institution's expansion. His early life showed signs of the accomplished scholar he would become. At a young age, he was a precocious reader and avid researcher. An intellectual curiosity and deep religious faith were an intertwined and reinforcing force throughout his teenage years. For Quinn, his questions about Mormonism did not betray a hidden doubt but rather pointed him towards research and study that would strengthen his belief. Before he entered college, Quinn had not only read the entire Bible, all the LDS scriptures, as well as early church publications, but had created indexes of each. He also carried out a line-by-line comparison of the 1830 Book of Mormon with other versions. Such efforts exhibited the devotion to study, intensity, and comprehensiveness he would bring to all his research.[16]

Quinn initially pursued a pre-med course of study as an undergraduate at Brigham Young University, but he soon devoted almost all his time to continuing his self-directed research into Mormonism. Quinn spent all the time he could in BYU's special collections library where he read through the original records of the LDS Church. Eventually, he switched his major to English literature. The road to academia was not clear cut, however. After having served a

---

15. Young, 31.
16. Topping, *D. Michael Quinn*, 9.

two-year mission to England, Quinn graduated from BYU in 1968 and enlisted in the military.[17]

Following three years in the armed services, Quinn enrolled in the history graduate program at the University of Utah in 1971. The timing was fortuitous as it coincided with the appointment of Apostle Howard Hunter to the role of Church Historian in 1970, which in turn marked the institution's increasing openness regarding its historical holdings. Hunter's immediate impact was to give historians wide access to the church archives, a monumental transformation of how the LDS Church had dealt with those who sought to research and write Mormon history. Quinn worked as a research assistant for his advisor, Davis Bitton, and later for Leonard Arrington, who replaced Hunter as Church Historian in 1972. Arrington, the author of 1958's landmark volume, *Great Basin Kingdom*, was the father of New Mormon History, of which Quinn would become a leading figure.[18] Quinn later argued that New Mormon History endeavored to "avoid using history as a religious battering ram."[19] By this he meant it neither sought to promote or discredit Mormonism itself, as an earlier generation of scholarship had, but to instead critically offer a humanistic, contextualized assessment of change over time.

This historiographic shift fit within and was shaped by larger intellectual developments in the U.S. history profession in the second half of the twentieth century. It was especially indebted to the rise of New History, an approach that moved away from grand narratives and "Great Man" theories, instead working for a cultural history that made more use of non-traditional sources and elevated the lives of overlooked historical subjects, especially women and people of color. But New Mormon History and its standard of an objective, professionalized approach to LDS history also depended on the wide-scale access allowed to church archives and the spirit of openness that characterized the LDS Church's attitude towards historical investigation in the 1970s. Bitton and others deemed this decade the

---

17. D. Michael Quinn, "My Journey From *Essentials in Church History* to *The Mormon Hierarchy* Series," *Journal of Mormon History* 44, no. 2 (April 2018): 61–62; Topping, *D. Michael Quinn*, 11–12, 20.

18. Quinn, "My Journey," 63–68; Topping, *D. Michael Quinn*, 23–32.

19. Quinn, "Editor's Introduction," viii.

"Camelot years," and Quinn later described the time as every day being like "Christmas morning."[20]

Rather than unwrapping Christmas presents, Quinn spent his days in the archives discovering things that had never been seen before as he opened boxes of early church documents. These included financial records, First Presidency minutes, diaries, and other personal papers. Quinn transcribed and catalogued the papers, creating an astonishing inventory that he and other historians would use for decades to come. This work as a researcher—which is often what he called himself in contrast to a historian—was monumental and path-breaking in itself. It was a contribution that would have altered the course of the study of Mormon history alone, to say nothing of the significance of the scholarship that Quinn produced from it.[21]

Such developments have usually been explained as part of the LDS Church's greater move towards both professionalization and greater openness and transparency in this period. Yet they were not unique to Mormonism, as they were happening within many different religious denominations in this era. Many examples exist of this, but the Catholic Church's Second Vatican Council provides the most powerful embodiment of the spirt of openness and reform coursing throughout American religious denominations at mid-century. Vatican II, as it was popularly known, was a series of meetings held by the Catholic bishops in Rome from 1962 to 1965 for the purposes of "updating" the church. Many things came out of this council, one of the most famous changes being the end of the Latin mass in exchange for the mass delivered in local languages. Other reforms allowed for the participation of the laity in the liturgy and the change of having the priest face the congregation during the mass rather than with his back to the audience. These adaptations signaled the Catholic Church's increasing openness, as well as the changing relationship of the church's hierarchy to its membership, something that found echoes within the LDS Church and other highly institutional denominations.[22]

---

20. Davis Bitton, "Ten Years in Camelot: A Personal Memoir," *Dialogue: A Journal of Mormon Thought* 16, no. 3 (Autum 1983): 9–20; David Haglund, "The Case of the Mormon Historian," *Slate*, Nov. 1, 2012, slate.com.

21. Topping, *D. Michael Quinn*, 24–27.

22. John W. O'Malley, *What Happened at Vatican II* (Cambridge, MA: Harvard University Press, 2008).

Similarly, the rising professionalization of the Church History office and throughout the LDS Church bureaucracy in this decade was mirrored by nearly every Christian denomination in the U.S. during these years. These turns towards professionalism were a result of religious groups' enormous growth since the 1950s, one which required more robust and stable institutional structures to manage the large memberships and maximize their potential. As denominational bureaucracies expanded, they staffed their ranks with specialized experts drawn from diverse fields, including history, sociology, accounting, marketing, psychology, and even international relations. This was a remarkable shift from the religiously trained leaders who had typically run American denominations.[23]

Quinn continued his graduate work at Yale University amid these noteworthy developments of American religious institutions and cultural change. He wrote his dissertation under Howard Lamar, the great historian of the American West. Quinn thrived in his academic endeavors at Yale while experiencing a crisis of faith, one brought about in part by his scholarly work. Quinn briefly considered quitting his doctoral study since it engaged sensitive information about the LDS Church, which he worried would harm the church and weaken his own faith. He even contemplated destroying his research, lest others find it and use it for ill purpose. But as he often did when faced with difficult circumstances, Quinn prayed about his decision and received a "spiritual witness" that he should continue his dissertation. Going forward, Quinn continued to "pray into print" everything he published.[24]

Quinn's dissertation, "The Mormon Hierarchy: An American Elite, 1832–1932," won two awards at Yale, including the prestigious Beinecke Dissertation prize. This research project was very much in line with Quinn's personal and intellectual preoccupations. It engaged questions about the LDS Church leadership that had interested him since a child, including his long-held frustration with how that leadership was often regarded as a monolithic body that

---

23. Conrad Wright, "The Growth of Denominational Bureaucracies: A Neglected Aspect of American Church History," *The Harvard Theological Review* 77, no. 2 (April 1984): p. 177–94.

24. Quinn, "On Being a Mormon Historian," 74.

acted as a uniform voice. From the church documents he had spent years reading, Quinn knew this wasn't the case. Instead, those records revealed the long history of internal dissension and disagreement among the church's leadership and showed the consequence of human actors. At the same time, Quinn's dissertation, like all intellectual projects, should also be understood in the context of its moment, a time of questioning and investigating American institutions in the post-Watergate environment. In this way, Quinn's project reflected a widespread scholarly skepticism of institutions, authority, and leadership, to say nothing of the larger cultural suspicions of American systems that were particularly prominent in the late 1970s.[25]

Despite the accolades and its zeitgeisty resonance, Quinn put his dissertation away for the time being, not publishing it as a book until almost twenty years later. Quinn, now a professor at BYU, likely understood how controversial his history of LDS leadership would be, especially as the LDS Church began to reverse its open attitude towards church history and its archives. Yet Quinn did not shy away from controversy altogether. His landmark 1985 essay, "LDS Church Authority and New Plural Marriages," his nearly one-hundred-page history of how Mormon polygamy continued after the 1890 Manifesto that forbade plural marriage was a daring act, perhaps even more risky than his dissertation topic.[26]

At the same time, Quinn should never be thought of as a scholar driven by provocation, but rather one inspired by historical problems. His exceptional book *Early Mormonism and the Magic World View* carried out a groundbreaking investigation of the role of folk magic and the supernatural in early nineteenth century New England, asking how these may have shaped Joseph Smith and his story of the Book of Mormon's origins.[27] The work grabbed the attention of religious scholars and nineteenth-century historians alike. Reviewing it for the *Pacific Historical Review*, the esteemed historian of Mormonism Newell Bringhurst called it "one of the most significant

25. Topping, *D. Michael Quinn*, 38–39; Benjamin E. Park, "The Life and Legacy of Michael Quinn," interview by Doug Fabrizio, *RadioWest*, Feb. 24, 2022, radiowest.kuer.org.

26. D. Michael Quinn, "LDS Church Authority and New Plural Marriages, 1890–1904," *Dialogue: A Journal of Mormon Thought* 18, no. 1 (Spring 1985): 9–105.

27. D. Michael Quinn, *Early Mormonism and the Magic World View* (Salt Lake City: Signature Books, 1987).

books yet written on Joseph Smith and early Mormon origins. It commands the attention of all students of Mormon history in particular and American religious history in general."[28] It would go on to win best book awards from the Mormon Historical Association and the John Whitmer Historical Association.

Quinn's publications and budding reputation happened under—and in spite of—increasing pressure from LDS Church authorities to make historical scholarship more faith promoting. The 1980s also saw the end of the "Camelot years," the brief period when the archives had been opened and objective and expansive historical research had been encouraged. Boyd K. Packer, a member of the Quorum of the Twelve Apostles, gave a searing address in 1981 to religious educators at BYU that marked this shift. Titled "The Mantle is Far, Far Greater than the Intellect," the talk offered an extended polemic of how history could be dangerous to the faith. Packer also highlighted the particular threat of church historians who, as he described, "write history as they were taught in graduate school, rather than as Mormons." Instead, it was the historian's obligation to present church history as a sacred story so that those who read or heard it would "see the hand of the Lord in every hour and moment of the Church from its beginning till now." Packer warned against what he saw as a human-centered or humanistic version of history, the very essence of the New Mormon History advanced by Quinn and others.[29]

Quinn delivered his response to Packer's talk not long after, also in a talk at BYU. The speech, titled "On Being a Mormon Historian," offered a point-by-point rebuttal to Packer's charges, dwelling especially on Packer's idea that there was no such thing as objective history. Quinn was offended by this notion, both as a scholar and as a person of faith. Countering this idea, Quinn attested to his own religious beliefs—something he would do frequently in his scholarship—and argued that these were fundamental to his work as a historian. Quinn particularly rejected Packer's suggestion that historians might be aiding the adversary by their work. The dogged

---

28. Newell G. Bringhurst, review of *Early Mormonism and the Magic World View*, *Pacific Historical Review* 58, no. 3 (August 1989): 380.

29. Boyd K. Packer, "The Mantle Is Far, Far Greater Than the Intellect," churchofjesuschrist.org.

historian instead maintained that by seeking historical truth, he was affirming the gospel, while simultaneously refraining from creating what he called "benignly angelic church leaders," which he believed would "border on idolatry." Quinn's address flipped Packer's argument on its head when he contended that the "so-called 'faith-promoting' church history which conceals controversies and difficulties of the Mormon past may actually undermine the faith of Latter-day Saints who eventually learn about the problems from other sources." Quinn's bold and brave assertion served not merely as a defense of objective historical methodology but also, he believed, of LDS faith.[30]

It was a risky move for a BYU professor to make, as the talk was perceived as a criticism of the LDS Church's leadership rather than an intellectual disagreement over the methods and merits of history. Through the 1980s, Quinn paid an increasing price for his rising public voice even as he earned tenure from BYU. He achieved promotion to full professorship and won the university's Outstanding Teacher award in 1986. But the clamps were coming down. The university started denying him research funds, refused sabbaticals, and pressured him not to publish his papers on controversial topics. Quinn finally resigned from BYU in 1988, unwilling to continue working under such limitations. Five years later, the LDS Church excommunicated the historian following the publication of his article, "Mormon Women Have Had the Priesthood Since 1843." Quinn was one of the "September Six," a group of intellectuals and feminists who were excommunicated or disfellowshipped over a span of thirteen days in 1993.[31]

Neither leaving BYU nor being excommunicated kept Quinn silent. Indeed, it seemed to have the opposite effect, perhaps emboldening and also releasing him to take up much of the work he would do in the following years. This was especially the case for his scholarship around sexuality and gender. The irony was that in the same years Quinn was becoming a pariah among LDS Church

---

30. Quinn, "On Being a Mormon Historian," 84, 87; Topping, *D. Michael Quinn*, 102–04.

31. Topping, *D. Michael Quinn*, 112–15, 118–19; Haglund, "Case of the Mormon Historian."

leaders, he was also becoming a minor media figure and rising public voice on Mormonism. This public profile began with the scuffle with Packer in 1981, an event that drew a full-page write-up by *Newsweek*'s respected religion journalist, Kenneth L. Woodward. In the article, "Apostles vs. Historians," Woodward pronounced Quinn "the most accomplished of the church's younger historians," and praised him for having provided a "stirring defense of intellectual integrity."[32] That media attention intensified with the coverage of the September Six's excommunications.[33] That America's major media outlets gave such visibility to these stories was no given, but rather reflected the enormous growing national interest in Mormonism in the 1980s. This interest was, in turn, shaped by other events including the Mark Hofmann scandal, the Mormon Tabernacle Choir's performance at Ronald Reagan's inauguration in 1981, and Reagan's 1982 trip to Utah where he praised the church's welfare program as a model for how religious institutions and the private sector, rather than the government, could best solve national problems.[34]

While both church authorities and biographers have, with varying purposes, noted Quinn's homosexuality, his life and scholarship have been insufficiently placed within the context of LGBTQ American history. The popular narrative of that history—and a good bit of the scholarship—has tended to treat the 1969 Stonewall Uprising, where queer persons fought back at law enforcement in a New York City gay bar, as a before-and-after dividing point that separates an earlier era of repression, discrimination, and social prohibition from the post-Stonewall decades that showed increasing visibility, the gaining of legal rights, and growing social acceptance for LGBTQ Americans.[35] But Quinn's life, like the lives of so many other LGBTQ people in these decades, complicates that neat

32. Kenneth L. Woodward, "Apostles Vs. Historians," *Newsweek*, Feb. 15, 1982, 77.

33. Dirk Johnson, "As Mormon Church Grows, So Does Dissent From Feminists and Scholars," *New York Times*, Oct. 2, 1993; Vern Anderson, "Mormon Dissidents Feel the Wrath of Church Elders," *Washington Post*, Oct. 16, 1993.

34. Young, *We Gather Together*, 229–30. See also, J. B. Haws, *The Mormon Image in the American Mind: Fifty Years of Public Perception* (New York: Oxford University Press, 2013), 99–157.

35. Dudley Clendinen and Adam Nagourney, *Out for Good: The Struggle to Build a Gay Rights Movement in America* (New York: Simon & Schuster, 1999).

"before and after," reminding us that no history is a story of linear progress—something his own scholarship on gay history within Mormonism demonstrates too.

Quinn said that he had been aware of a different sexual identity from as early as the age of eight.[36] Thanks to his research, we know that the years of his dawning sexual awareness were happening at the very same time in which the LDS Church gave increasing attention to the "sin" of homosexuality, something that Quinn showed was a departure from an earlier history of Mormon tolerance or disinterest in same-sex sexuality.[37] Quinn identified 1952 as the time when he started to become aware of his sexuality—the same year that the LDS Church made its first ever public pronouncement on homosexuality, deeming it an "abomination." Six years later, Bruce R. McConkie's *Mormon Doctrine*, an influential compendium of beliefs and practices, listed homosexuality as a sin. LDS Church teachings and materials prescribed heterosexual marriage as a "cure" for homosexuality and brutal "aversion therapy" treatments were developed for those who expressed same-sex attraction into the 1960s. In 1968, for instance, the revised Church Handbook of Instructions made homosexuality an excommunicable offense. Such developments underscore the intensifying anti-homosexual theology and institutional practices that happened across Quinn's formational years as an adolescent and young man, developments that the astute and attentive Quinn likely was especially aware of and shaped by.[38]

Importantly, LDS belief systems and religious teachings about homosexuality were shaped within a larger cultural and political context at mid-century America known as the Lavender Scare. This was a time when the federal government singled out homosexuals as a threat to national security because they were believed to be easily turned into communist spies. The federal government, the FBI, and

36. Topping, *D. Michael Quinn*, 5–6.

37. D. Michael Quinn, *Same-Sex Dynamics among Nineteenth-Century Americans: A Mormon Example* (Urbana: University of Illinois Press, 1996), and, "Prelude to the National 'Defense of Marriage' Campaign: Civil Discrimination against Feared or Despised Minorities," *Dialogue: A Journal of Mormon Thought* 33, no. 3 (Fall 2000): 1–52.

38. Neil J. Young, "Homosexuality and Politics in Mormonism," in Amy Hoyt and Taylor G. Petrey, eds. *The Routledge Handbook of Mormonism and Gender* (London and New York: 2020), 206–07.

local law enforcement in cities across the country targeted, harassed, surveilled, and imprisoned thousands of homosexuals during the 1950s and 1960s.[39] Against that political and legal backdrop, almost every American religious denomination developed anti-homosexual theologies and policies. This was not unique to Mormonism but rather part of a consensus religious world view being created in this period about homosexuality seen throughout almost the entire swath of American Christianity. The LDS Church's surveillance of its own suspected homosexual members, including Quinn, may have been unique among American religious institutions, however. Indeed, several years before his excommunication, Quinn had learned he was being surveilled by security teams from both BYU and LDS Church headquarters, looking to catch him in a compromising situation.[40]

At the same time, queer people of faith began advocating for themselves as believers. Gay and lesbian persons of faith refused to accept excommunication, religious shunning, and theological condemnations as definitive responses to their lives. Some created their own religious institutions, such as the Metropolitan Community Church, an LGBTQ-affirming denomination founded by Rev. Troy Perry in Huntington Beach, California, in 1968. Within various religious denominations, gay Christians formed their own support groups, such as Dignity, an organization for gay Catholics founded in 1969. Similarly, queer Latter-day Saints organized Affirmation during a gay rights conference held in Salt Lake City in 1977.[41] It seems noteworthy that Quinn was delivering the keynote address at an Affirmation conference in San Diego while his disciplinary council was being held in 1993.[42] In maintaining his LDS faith for the rest of his life, despite his excommunication, Quinn fits within this larger history of queer American believers who held on to their religious faith and navigated their religious belonging in different ways.

---

39. David K. Johnson, *The Lavender Scare: The Cold War Persecution of Gays and Lesbians in the Federal Government* (Chicago: The University of Chicago Press, 2004).

40. Topping, *D. Michael Quinn*, 112.

41. Heather R. White, *Reforming Sodom: Protestants and the Rise of Gay Rights* (Chapel Hill: The University of North Carolina Press, 2015), 140–41; Paul Mortensen, "Affirmation——In the Beginning," affirmation.org.

42. Haglund, "Case of the Mormon Historian."

As Quinn once said, "I'm a seventh-generation Mormon. Nothing can take that away from me."[43]

This cultural, political, and religious history of homosexuality in the second half of the twentieth century must be recognized in understanding Quinn's decision to enter into marriage with his wife, Jan, in 1967, his coming out to her in 1972, and their marriage lasting until 1985.[44] Their union not only followed LDS recommendations about what those who experienced "same-sex attractions" ought to do to "cure" them, but resembled thousands of other American marriages in these years where a homosexual person, usually a man, was counseled by his religious faith leaders to pursue heterosexual marriage in order to suppress or subvert their homosexuality.[45] In this milieu, Quinn's coming out to Jan in 1972 would have meant something much different than our contemporary conceptions of that event, which typically understand "coming out" as a public declaration of an outward identity that is lived out. For Quinn, his 1972 conversation likely resulted from his lifelong commitment to honesty and personal integrity.

Yet we should also understand how, in the years just shortly after Stonewall, many gay Americans still understood that "coming out" meant a process of internal recognition of one's sexuality and, sometimes, the sharing of that knowledge with a select number of trusted others.[46] Quinn may not have been personally motivated by the events of Stonewall and the nascent gay rights movement taking shape in the early 1970s. Yet the arc from his private conversation with Jan in 1972 to his eventual public living as a gay man following their 1985

---

43. Tad Walch, "D. Michael Quinn, Who Wrote 10 Books on Latter-day Saint History, Dies at 77," *Deseret News*, Apr. 24, 2021, deseret.com.

44. Topping, *D. Michael Quinn*, 20.

45. Neil J. Young, "Mormons and Same-Sex Marriage: From ERA to Prop 8," in Patrick Q. Mason and John G. Turner, eds., *Out of Obscurity: Mormonism since 1945* (New York: Oxford University Press, 2016), 148. See also, Rebecca L. Davis, "'My Homosexuality Is Getting Worse Every Day: Norman Vincent Peale, Psychiatry, and the Liberal Protestant Response to Same-Sex Desires in Mid-Twentieth Century America," in Catherine A. Brekus and W. Clark Gilpin, eds., *American Christianities: A History of Dominance and Diversity* (Chapel Hill: The University of North Carolina Press, 2011), 347–65; and White, *Reforming Sodom*, 27–28.

46. Abigail C. Saguy, *Come Out, Come Out, Whoever You Are* (New York: Oxford University Press, 2020), 11–16.

separation aligns almost perfectly with the same personal trajectories of thousands of other gay and lesbian Americans in these years.

Quinn's writing of his landmark 1996 book, *Same-Sex Dynamics among Nineteenth-Century Americans: A Mormon Example*, has often been described as being made possible by his public coming out and his official separation from the LDS Church. However, it ought to also be understood in the context of the rise of Queer Studies in the 1980s and 1990s and the flourishing of LGBTQ historical scholarship in this period. *Same-Sex Dynamics*, which showed that in the nineteenth century and early twentieth century the LDS Church generally tolerated Latter-day Saints who engaged in a "range of same-sex dynamics," made a groundbreaking contribution to that literature.[47] More than any other of his works, it also introduced Quinn to the widest breadth of scholars, including from the disciplines of history, religion, American studies, and gender and sexuality studies.

While a path-breaking work of scholarship, *Same-Sex Dynamics* also reveals itself as very much a product of its historical moment. It was clearly shaped by the roiling politics of gay rights in the 1990s that saw important advancements, like the million-person March on Washington for Lesbian, Gay, and Bi Equal Rights in 1993, and disastrous setbacks, especially Congress' passage of the Defense of Marriage Act in 1996. Even more than its contents, much of the critical response to Quinn's book showed the influence of the times. One common criticism was that the book's "same-sex dynamics" didn't always include same-sex sexual activity, thus invalidating Quinn's thesis. Yet such commentary showed a late twentieth-century, post-Stonewall perspective of homosexuality that treated sexual identity as synonymous with sexual activity. In this way, by projecting a modern expectation of homosexuality onto these nineteenth century subjects, Quinn's critics unwittingly revealed their contemporary conceptions about sexuality rather than providing a useful analysis of Quinn's investigation. Some LDS critics even tried to discredit *Same-Sex Dynamics* by arguing that Quinn's sexual orientation disqualified him as an objective voice. Writing for *FARMS Review*, the Mormon reviewers George Mitton and Rhett James

---

47. Quinn, *Same-Sex Dynamics*, 2.

repeatedly referred to Quinn's "homosexual agenda" in writing the book they deemed a "homosexual distortion of Latter-day Saint history."[48] The phrase, "homosexual agenda," had gained increasing usage among political conservatives in the 1990s, although usually amended as a "radical homosexual agenda." Notably, in using such language, Quinn's LDS critics had drawn from the political discourse of 1990s conservatism to assess the book's historical claims.

Academic appraisers responded to the book far more favorably. *Same-Sex Dynamics* won the American Historical Association's 1997 Herbert Feis Award given to the best book written by an independent scholar.[49] In her review of *Same-Sex Dynamics* for the *Journal of American History*, the historian Anne M. Butler praised Quinn's book as "sterling scholarship, balanced interpretation, and insightful analysis." Considering its impressive research, Butler observed, "Rarely does one encounter a work as meticulously documented as this. ... Quinn finds the extensive evidence that supports his thesis."[50]

Yet throughout his career, the scale and scope of Quinn's research and documentation, hardly a unique feature of *Same-Sex Dynamics*, have not always been regarded positively by his academic peers. For example, almost a decade earlier, Newell G. Bringhurst's otherwise favorable assessment of *Early Mormonism and the Magic World View* complained that the book was "written in a pedantic, dissertation-like manner and contains frequent, lengthy footnotes encased within the text itself which disturb the flow of the story."[51] Bringhurst was far from the only one to offer such comments on Quinn's research and writing style.

Although this essay has considered Quinn's life and work within the broadest contexts of American history, I want to, in closing, use some of Quinn's own words to rethink—or at least complicate—the frequent view of Quinn's scholarship that criticized it as overly

---

48. George L. Mitton and Rhett S. James, "A Response to D. Michael Quinn's Homosexual Distortion of Latter-day Saint History," *FARMS Review* 10, no. 1 (1998): 144, 175, 189. See also, Klaus J. Hansen, "Quinnspeak," *FARMS Review* 10, no. 1 (1998): 132–40.

49. "In Remembrance: D. Michael Quinn '76PhD," *Yale Alumni Magazine*, yale-alumnimagazine.org.

50. Anne M. Butler, review of *Same-Sex Dynamics among Nineteenth-Century Americans, Journal of American History* 84, no. 1 (June 1997): 239.

51. Bringhurst, review of *Early Mormonism*, 380.

researched or pedantically written. In his memoir, Quinn reflected on how the crisis of his parents' divorce and especially his—at the time—five-years-old perception of having caused it substantively shaped his personal and emotional development. "I spent the rest of my life trying to be the perfect son, the righteous Mormon, the good student and the perpetually nice guy in order to earn people's love and respect," Quinn wrote. "I felt there was something wrong deep inside me."[52]

Such thinking surely also was molded by his youthful recognition of his different sexuality within a nation and religious faith that both regarded homosexuality as an affliction of the sick and the sinful. Whatever the life events that shaped such a psychology, Quinn's pressure of perfection should be recognized as manifesting not only in his temperament but also in the texts he produced. In his lengthy articles and books and in their voluminous footnotes, many of which stretched across several pages, his tendency towards over-documentation must have been a result of the perfectionist penchant that always dogged him. Given the enormous pressures upon him, both internal and external, Quinn's exhaustive research and his thorough presentation likely assured him that he had done the necessary work to make some of the most original, important, and controversial claims of Mormon historiography. Additionally, his footnotes are the roadmaps of investigation left for other scholars to trace. Certainly all of us who do Mormon history owe Quinn a great debt of gratitude for how scrupulously he plotted the pathways for our own inquiries.

In 1972, while having just started graduate school but already with many years of research under his belt, Quinn recorded in his journal his thoughts about this endeavor. "For over a decade[,] I have researched out areas—problem areas—in LDS Church history, so that I might understand them thoroughly and be able to explain them with honesty and love," Quinn wrote.[53] Over and over again, Quinn accomplished this task, even as personal, institutional, and religious obstacles seemed to conspire to deter such efforts. As scholars continue to evaluate the significant contributions of Quinn's

52. D. Michael Quinn, "Chosen Path: A Gay Chicano's Odyssey in Mormon History," quoted in Topping, *D. Michael Quinn*, 7.
53. Quinn, "My Journey," 67.

oeuvre to the literature of Mormon history, we might all do better to recognize how this practice of "honesty and love" was the consistent characteristic of his methodology—and, especially, how we each might make it core to our own.

D. Michael Quinn: A Personal Remembrance

GARY JAMES BERGERA

Mike Quinn (1944–2021) stands as one of the preeminent historians of the Church of Jesus Christ of Latter-day Saints of the last quarter of the twentieth century. His stature, contributions, and impact were singular during those years. For many readers of the period, among whom I include myself, Quinn personified the emerging New Mormon History movement: fresh, exhilarating, exciting. He was probing, articulate, and thoughtful; his access to and knowledge of the historical sources were deep and far-reaching. On a personal level, he could be captivating, engaging, charming. I don't believe there had been another Mormon historian of his caliber before him, and so far I haven't yet seen another historian of his exceptional impact.

In this brief essay, I'd like to share a few personal reminiscences of Quinn, including from the point of view of someone who worked with him as an editor, in order to offer some thoughts regarding his relationship and contributions to what has become known as the New Mormon History. From late 1984 to 2000, I directed Signature Books, one of his publishers. Then, from 2001 to the end of 2022, I managed the Smith-Pettit Foundation. In both positions, I interacted with Quinn on professional and personal levels dealing notably with his scholarship and writing. I should add that my own relationship with Quinn was complicated but almost always rewarding. On the one hand, I admired, respected, liked him immensely. At other times he was annoying, infuriating, and drove me crazy, and we both promised we would never again work with each another—a vow we repeatedly broke.

As a historian, Quinn was a tireless, exhaustive researcher. His occasional full-page footnotes became the stuff of legend; it seemed as though he ever met a footnote he couldn't make longer. In his use

23

of documentation, he was careful, insightful, and often correct. He was not infallible, but one disagreed with his conclusions at one's own risk. As a writer, he felt strongly about his use of words, grammar, punctuation, and syntax. When he disagreed with the editing of his texts, he could be argumentative to the point of bullying, with his comments to the editor often upper-cased, underlined, lecturing, condescending. He was stubborn and sometimes obdurate to his own detriment. He tended to resist help when, in my opinion, it clearly benefited his work.

Yet at the same time, Quinn expressed deep-seated insecurities in his abilities as a writer. He often compared himself to the world's great authors and, as a result, lamented that he could never measure up to their standard. In fact, a general, overarching tendency to self-criticism riddled aspects of his life. For example, he was convinced, both during his marriage and after his divorce, that he had failed as a husband and father, insisting that some of his critics at LDS Church-owned Brigham Young University were better men—better husbands and fathers—than he. Quinn was deeply scarred emotionally and psychologically—more, I believe, than he himself acknowledged—by his childhood and adolescence especially. The causes were varied, but included his father's attempts to recast his life, not as Hispanic, but as Anglo, as well as his grandmother's misandry and erotophobia, and his church's homophobia and anti-gay policies.[1]

As a public figure, intellectual, and role model, Quinn usually exuded confidence, intelligence, poise, and equanimity. He was friendly, disarming, encouraging, and genuinely interested in others. More than a few of his students and admirers loved him. When he resigned from BYU in 1988, at age forty-four, he expected to easily find employment elsewhere. However, it turned out that he had miscalculated and that his expectations were too high. He had at least two opportunities to teach at community colleges but declined both

---

1. Quinn's posthumously published memoir, *Chosen Path* (Salt Lake City: Signature Books, forthcoming), addresses in detail these aspects of his upbringing as well as his responses to the LDS Church's position on homosexuality. On the latter, see also his book-length history *Same-Sex Dynamics among Nineteenth-Century Americans: A Mormon Example* (Urbana: University of Illinois Press, 2001), and his "Prelude to the National 'Defense of Marriage' Campaign: Civil Discrimination Against Feared or Despised Minorities," *Dialogue: A Journal of Mormon Thought* 33, no. 3 (Fall 2000): 1–52.

because he found the teaching loads too heavy and the salaries too low. Other academic opportunities in which he was more interested proved to be unreachable due to personal and political controversies.[2] And he refused to seek employment outside the academy, fearing that such jobs would adversely impact his ability to teach and research again.

Following his departure from BYU, Quinn lived from fellowship to fellowship, from writing contract to writing contract, and from credit card to credit card until his deceased mother's estate and his own social security benefits afforded him a modicum of comfort. From about 2010 on, when he realized that he would never teach again, his scholarly output slowed considerably. I would be surprised to learn that any of the projects he had worked on during his final decade were anywhere near completion, except as possibly expanded revisions of previously published works.

Quinn preferred to describe himself as a "DNA Mormon," even after his expulsion from the LDS Church in 1993. His continuing belief in the truth claims of the LDS Church may be difficult for some people to understand, let alone accept, given the church's treatment of him as well as his own generally liberal, non-judgmental approach to life.[3] Yet his belief in the fundamentals of Mormonism were unshaken: a testimony that God lives, that Jesus died for the sins of humanity, that God continues to speak to his children, that Joseph Smith was God's prophet and the Book of Mormon God's book were, in fact, as real for him as any "objective" event in history. Quinn was genuinely convinced that his controversial works of Mormon history not only served the LDS Church's best long-term interests, but, as may be seen in some of the quotations in this essay, were sanctioned by God according to God's direct revelation to him.

---

2. See, for example, Daniel Golden, "In Religious Studies, Universities Bend to Views of Faithful," *Wall Street Journal*, Apr. 6, 2006, at wsj.com.

3. See Lavina Fielding Anderson, "DNA Mormon: D. Michael Quinn," in *Mormon Mavericks: Essays on Dissenters*, ed. John Sillito and Susan Staker (Salt Lake City: Signature Books, 2002), 329–63; and D. Michael Quinn, "On Being a Mormon Historian (and Its Aftermath)," in *Faithful History: Essays on Writing Mormon History*, ed. George D. Smith (Salt Lake City: Signature Books, 1992), 69–111 (published a year before his excommunication). For a consideration of Quinn as a historian, see Gary Topping, *D. Michael Quinn: Mormon Historian* (Salt Lake City: Signature Books, 2022).

To my mind, Quinn's greatest contributions to scholarship are five-fold. Each is important in its own right; together they attest to his enduring legacy within the broader scholarly and Mormon communities.

First, Quinn was unquestionably the standard bearer for the New Mormon History. He was neither the first nor the only New Mormon Historian. But for many of us, he represented the very best of the New Mormon History's emphasis on balance, transparency, honesty, generosity, and adherence to the historical records. While the term New Mormon History originally meant to embrace a multi-disciplinary approach to the study of the Mormon past, it has, since the 1960s, come to refer more broadly to approaches that reflect greater access to and reliance on the original manuscript sources; that display greater nuance and compassion of interpretation—interpretations that are not tied to binary judgments of pro- and anti-Mormonism, religious and secular, theistic and atheistic, but rather exhibit an appreciation and championing of multi-faceted approaches. While traditionalist Mormon historians—those grounded in a strict dichotomy of pro- and anti—may have viewed the advent of the New Mormon History with concern, even alarm, the New Mormon History has achieved growing acceptance among an increasingly educated, increasingly internet-connected LDS Church membership. Quinn stood among the avant garde of the New Mormon Historians, and his published contributions to Mormon history moved the scholarly and respectability bar much higher.[4]

Second, Quinn may be the most dogged, probing, unrelenting researcher of the Mormon past who ever lived.[5] For years, he spent hours daily transcribing and taking verbatim notes from the historical records of the LDS Church Historian's Office/Historical Department and other repositories. (I still vividly recall seeing his padlocked file cabinets in his office at BYU safeguarding his thousands of pages of typed transcriptions of original documents past historians could only have dreamed of accessing.) He described

---

4. For an overview of Quinn's scholarship, especially his books, see Topping, *Quinn*, chaps. 4–7.

5. His only rival may be Andrew Jenson (1850–1941), an early twentieth-century LDS historian. See Andrew Jenson, *A Historian in Zion: The Autobiography of Andrew Jenson, Assistant Church Historian*, eds. Reid L. Nielson and R. Mark Melville (Salt Lake City: Deseret Book Co., 2016).

himself during these years as a Mormon monk. More than anyone else before him and for years after him, Quinn benefitted from the openness that LDS Apostle and Church Historian Howard W. Hunter inaugurated at LDS headquarters beginning in 1970. Other historians were, and are, equally exemplary scholars. But Quinn's access to and knowledge of the Mormon past seemed preternatural. While he was usually reluctant to make his research materials available to other writers, I'm aware of instances when he occasionally shared his extensive notes on specific topics with other researchers.[6]

Third, Quinn may be the most honest Mormon historian ever. I don't mean to suggest that other historians were or are not as honest. But I don't believe there was ever a topic Quinn shied away from. In fact, if Quinn ever felt pressure, from himself or others, not to explore a particular topic, such pressure merely served to further energize and propel his research interests. Consider, for example, the following two excerpts from Quinn's memoir, *Chosen Path*, regarding the preparation and possible publication of his master's thesis, a group study of the LDS hierarchy, completed at the University of Utah in 1973. At the time, Quinn had worked for the LDS Church Historical Department, reporting directing to the first academically credentialed official Church Historian, Leonard J. Arrington. (Arrington was almost fifty-six; Quinn twenty-nine.)

> From my journal: "He [Leonard Arrington] said that nobody has ever attempted what I am in the process of doing regarding the Mormon hierarchy. He said that the material I present, especially in the 3rd chapter, is like a barrage of unrelenting gunfire or like the constant dripping of the Chinese water torture. Without some kind of change, he said, the effect was devastating. ...
>
> "He indirectly suggested that I not submit my work on the hierarchy as a Master's Thesis, but instead print portions of it in larger studies.
>
> "As Leonard spoke, I sat leaning on my typewriter[,] listening and saying nothing. When he had finished, I reminded him that I had worked two years on the thesis and I had every intention of graduating with my

---

6. For an insider's view of the early days of the LDS Church Historical Department, see Leonard J. Arrington, *Adventures of a Mormon Historian* (Urbana: University of Illinois Press, 1998), 55–92.

M.A. I said [that] I '*had*' to finish my M.A. … [and] that I would have to do [its thesis as] my prosopographical study on the hierarchy."

I aspired to be the Sir Lewis Namier of Mormon studies, but Mormonism's first professionally trained Church Historian wanted me to go beyond that. As I wrote this day: "Leonard seems to be more than a little concerned about the reverberations that will result from my thesis." …

From my journal: "He had me meet with him and Davis [Bitton, LDS Church Assistant Historian and one of Quinn's professors at the University of Utah] to discuss the issue. … I became increasingly concerned that he was regarding my thesis as a product of HDC [Historical Department of the Church] rather than a graduate thesis. I said [that] I did not feel I should be penalized in my use of sources merely because of my position with HDC.

"I resented the possibility that I might not be allowed to use sources which even non-members have had access to. I also spoke about my concern that my thesis might be emasculated. Davis agreed with me[,] but I could tell [that] Leonard was becoming irritated.

"He was so agitated that[,] instead of addressing me, he directed remarks for my benefit to Davis. Thus, Leonard said to Davis[,] 'Now, if this was me, I would appreciate someone watching out for my interests' and later he exclaimed: 'Doesn't he trust us to review his thesis without acting as censors?' I tried to mollify the situation, and felt very bad that I had angered Leonard. However, I felt it necessary to express some of my concerns.["] …

I left [Arrington's office] this day with a profound awareness that my commitment to full disclosure in writing the history of the LDS Church was more extreme than the kind of "openness" Leonard advocated. The "New Mormon History" meant something different to me than it did to Leonard Arrington, its chief architect.[7]

Fourth, Quinn's painstaking, dense studies of the upper ecclesiastical echelons of the LDS Church, including his expanded biography of J. Reuben Clark (a longtime member of the church's First Presidency), are master classes in historical narrative and, in my opinion, will probably never be surpassed. Quinn's other two book-length studies—on Mormonism and magic and Mormonism and same-sex issues—were similarly important. But his three-volume history of the Mormon hierarchy reflects a profoundly informed, meticulously studied analysis

---

7. See Quinn, *Chosen Path*, June 8 and July 6, 1973, entries.

that in terms of scope and depth is breathtaking. (That readers today may not be as impressed, shocked even, speaks to the gradual infiltration of Quinn's work in the LDS intellectual environment. What was once shocking is now mundane.) The practical realities of the academy today would probably never permit such a decades-spanning consumption of staff time, money, and energy. In truth, however, what drove Quinn was not so much professional acclaim—though Quinn's ego was not immune to recognition and flattery—as religious calling. Much as medieval builders saw their churches and cathedrals as tangible expressions of their faith in God, so Quinn treated his histories as literal testaments of his belief in the LDS Church.

Fifth, and finally, Quinn's explorations of LGBTQ Mormon history in both a book and articles helped to map new territory in the study of Mormon history. While there had been forays into Mormonism's queer past before—Connell O'Donovan's important 1994 essay, "The Abominable and Detestable Crime Against Nature," was the best study prior to Quinn's 1996 *Same-Sex Dynamics among Nineteenth-Century Americans*[8]—Quinn brought to bear on the topic an encyclopedic knowledge of both the historical sources and the historical contexts. His approach was sensitive; his analysis cautious, even conservative; and his investment personal, non-confrontational. However much scholars may quibble over some of Quinn's conclusions, his work represented an insightful, invigorating engagement with important elements of the Mormon past. All future studies of the topic owe major debts to Quinn's efforts.

I'd like to close by quoting three excerpts from Quinn's memoir, *Chosen Path*. Quinn's picaresque autobiography, drawn from his diaries, other contemporary documents, as well as his own memories, is structured as a heavily annotated chronology. The first entry I'd like to share is dated April 26, 1973. Prior to this day, Quinn had filled an LDS proselytizing mission in England, married Janet Darley in 1967, graduated in English from Brigham Young University in 1969, served three years in the US Army in Germany, then started

---

8. O'Donovan's essay appeared in *Multiply and Replenish: Essays on Mormon Sex and Family*, ed. Brent D. Corcoran (Salt Lake City: Signature Books, 1994), 123–70. A revised, expanded version is available at connellodonovan.com. Quinn's book was published by the University of Illinois Press.

his master's program in history at the University of Utah. In the excerpt below, Quinn is completing his graduate studies, preparing to end his employment at the LDS Church Historical Department, and contemplating the beginning of a doctoral program in history at Yale University. He is taking stock of his life, of his motivations, of what he hopes to accomplish, and of some of the challenges ahead.

At every stage [in researching and writing Mormon history], I asked God's guidance for me to know how to tell "the truth in love." I felt that this would be a strength to Mormons and a resource for LDS leaders.

Yet it's fair to ask why I chose to research and write about controversial topics of the Mormon past? At the time, I felt that I was simply trying to understand problem areas and provide a means for faithful understanding.

But I now realize that there were subconscious factors operating in my choices as a Mormon historian. First, I sought out areas of apparent ambiguity or contradiction in the LDS Church's past and tried to resolve them. That was something I hadn't been able to do with the ambiguity and contradiction within me.

Second, I now recognize that I saw my father reflected in the Church's official concealment of its controversial past. I was as determined to uncover the secrets of the Mormon past, as I was to discover those of my father's Mexican heritage. After all, the leaders of the LDS Church had been an earthly father-substitute for most of my life.

Third, I now also realize that I saw the LDS Church in my exact situation—outwardly happy and prospering, but burdened with unspoken secrets and wounds that needed to be opened for the process of healing and health. Guess I hoped to obtain some vicarious comfort by bringing a resolution for the Mormon experience that I couldn't give to my own life.

While I must admit that there has been a lot of subconscious "projection" in my choices as a Mormon historian, I have always done my best to recreate the Mormon experience as accurately and fully as the available sources allowed. I have hoped that Jesus, Joseph, and Brigham would approve of my efforts. I still do, even though current LDS leaders would eventually make it clear that they didn't like my stirring up the past. Another echo of Dad.

I cite this entry because it encapsulates Quinn as both person and scholar. It is honest, even raw, in ways almost never encountered in Mormon biography. Quinn was writing to be read, and he knew that his honesty and transparency could be used in ways he did not intend. Still, he persisted in such acts of deliberate self-disclosure—and there are entries in Quinn's memoir that some readers may find too jarring, as if one were inadvertently eavesdropping on a too-intimate conversation or witness a too-private act—convinced that the truth of one's existence was ultimately its own *raison d'être*.

The second excerpt from Quinn's memoir is dated January 22, 1980. Here, he is coming to terms that neither he nor God will ever change his sexuality, his marriage is increasingly sexless and is unraveling, and he knows that his future as a professor of history at BYU, where he has been employed for the past three and a half years, is uncertain. His agonizing choice is whether to suppress his nature and be miserable, rendering everyone else around him similarly miserable, or accept his nature and live with the consequences, hoping that in any event he, and others, will be happier. Quinn's pain, as he contemplates such a decision, is nearly unbearable.

> I loved God, the Church, and the flesh, and I felt that by repressing the third love[,] I would find complete fulfillment in acceptable ways through the first two loves. ... Could the destructive results of choosing the way of the carnality that was natural for me from ages ten to eighteen have been any worse than the ultimate damage I have caused, am causing, and will cause by rejecting those carnal options and seeking to be a spiritual Mormon, husband, father, potential Apostle and god-in-embryo? ...
>
> I honestly wonder if I had taken the many possible roads to the [homosexual] sensuality that was natural to me, if the outcome could have made me more miserable than I am now. I don't think that I could have felt as bad about the unhappiness such a course would have brought to my family as I now feel about the unhappiness it has brought to my wife and will ultimately bring to my family anyway.
>
> The road I have taken has expanded the circle of misery without enabling me to do a lot of good in the lives of others. ... I cannot recapture that lost option, because if I now took the opportunity (such as it is) for the sensual life I have rejected for twenty-five years, it would not undo the shambles of my present life and it would not bring much sexual contentment either (since I am now nearly asexual, burned-out by repression).

I look at myself, what I am and what it is logical that I can expect to be, and I ask: Has it been worth all of the above for me to be a revisionist writer of LDS history, a silver-tongued orator at occasional Church meetings, and an inadequate and indifferent low-level Church administrator? God only knows, and I am in His hands as I have always wanted to be. *Quo Vadis*—should that be a declaration or a question of my life?

… how many [LDS marriages] are like mine? God have mercy on those of us who have failed so miserably while trying so hard to [be] good and fulfill Your will!

Quinn's resolution was to divorce, leave BYU, look for employment elsewhere, and hope for a long-term significant, loving relationship. I don't know that he ever seriously entertained second thoughts about his decision. I know that he would have liked full-time employment in the academy, albeit on his conditions. While he still struggled—money, relationships, career, writing projects, housing, etc.—he always seemed mostly happier, more contented after he left Utah.

The third and final excerpt is from his memoirs' conclusion. Quinn is now in his mid-sixties, is twenty-plus years away from BYU, and has never been able to secure full-time employment nor enjoy a long-term relationship. He realizes that he has essentially exhausted all avenues for a career at a university. He is on social security and lives in the condominium he inherited from his mother. While some may be tempted to regard Quinn's life at this point as tragic, I want to believe they are wrong. That Quinn may have hoped for more should not be read as failure. Quinn knew that he had made significant contributions to better understanding the Mormon past; he knew that he had been a pillar of the New Mormon History; he knew that as both a teacher and historian, he had impacted for the better the lives of countless students and readers; and he knew that his singular impact on the Mormon intellectual community and environment would outlive him. He may have wanted more and other things, but he accepted the consequences of his decisions.

With their emphasis on the path of Mormonism I chose, these already-too-long memoirs have neglected my efforts since the late 1980s to explore male-male intimacy. This Unchartered Terrain deserves as much attention as my Chosen Path, especially since the two were intertwined from my mid-forties onward.

Because these memoirs avoid the first, they have skipped years-at-a-time after I resigned from BYU's faculty. And merely skim over the important events in my dwindling path of choice since 1987. I admit that there should be a post-1987 narrative as detailed as these memoirs are for the earlier period.

Still, I want to delay such an account until I've had a long-term relationship of love and intimacy with another male. My old man's version of what gay lovers and young Evangelical troubadours Jason and DeMarco sing about in their album *Till the End of Time*.

I would like to think of this future boyfriend looking over my shoulder as I chronicle our first meeting. We might even call each other "Husband."

Then he can write the conclusion in his own words. Like the gay-boy's song to his aging male-lover: "I'll Follow You Into the Dark."

It won't matter if he's not a Mormon in background or belief. It might be easier for us both if he isn't.

God knows.

Mike Quinn died alone at home of an apparent heart attack sometime around April 21, 2021. He had turned seventy-seven less than a month earlier. News of his death was more than unexpected; it was shocking, surreal. He had seemed to be in reasonably good health. Even now, I find it easy to think of him attending and speaking at an upcoming historical conference, swapping interesting tidbits of the Mormon past, sharing his opinions of current movies, lecturing editors on how to edit. That none of these will happen seems impossible. Quinn was and remains one of heaven's extraordinary, complicated creations. His death leaves a permanent void in the universe.

The *Straight*jacket of Time: Narrating D. Michael Quinn

SARA M. PATTERSON

The snow may never slush upon the hillside.
By nine p.m. the moonlight must appear.
In short, there's simply not
A more congenial spot
For happily-ever-aftering than here in Camelot.[1]

The lyrics capture the premise of the story: they claim that Camelot is a perfect and ordered place. Yet as we quickly learn, the idyllic Camelot, untouched by disorder or calamity, cannot be sustained because of human flaws. When called "Camelot," Leonard Arrington's reign as Church Historian, and Mike Quinn's promising place in it, suggest a past that was Edenic, a past that could yet return, a past in which historians and the church are not imagined at odds with one another. While the once and hoped-for future Camelot is but one narrative in which we have trapped Mike Quinn, it certainly isn't the only one. As historians and lovers of history, we need to free Mike Quinn from the linear chains in which we've bound him. Two narratives in particular hold him hostage: the martyr narrative and the narrative *straight*jacket of capitalist hetero- and theo-normativity. In this essay I explore both entrapment narratives and suggest that perhaps the best way to understand Quinn and his life lies in the concept of queer time, a notion that will liberate Quinn and memories of him from his captors.

The first of the narratives holding him hostage is the martyr narrative present in the discourse around Quinn, especially among

---

1. Alan Lerner and Frederick Loewe, "Camelot," *Camelot*, original cast recording, 1961, lyrics at lyrics.com.

liberal and progressive Mormons. One classic example of this is Lavina Fielding Anderson's, "DNA Mormon: D. Michael Quinn" in *Mormon Mavericks: Essays on Dissenters*. Take, for example, her discussion of Quinn's life:

> Michael is a gay man in a church whose "love gays" rhetoric can only be described as the foam on a wave of deep fear and mistrust of homosexuals. Economically, Michael's prosperous, even brilliant academic career was shattered around him. His marriage ended in divorce. His enormous love for and pride in his children was complicated not only by this divorce from Jan and by the agony of his son Adam's suicide but also by religious division. Michael, excommunicated, still loves and believes in Mormonism, even though he finds church attendance emotionally difficult. In contrast, his children find nothing relevant in Mormonism and Jan resigned from the church soon after the excommunications.[2]

In just a few short sentences, Anderson captures the all-encompassing nature of the martyr narrative told about Quinn. Here his life is recounted as a series of losses, each one contextualized within a broader narrative about his social ostracization from his church community and divisions from his family, alongside a deep and abiding grief about the loss of his son. Anderson's narrative about Quinn is captivating precisely because it characterizes the losses he suffered through the lens of a larger meaningful goal of following the truth wherever it would lead.

It seems that at times even Quinn understood his own experiences as a type of martyrdom as well, knowing that the outcome of publishing the truth about a history that the institutional church would rather keep silent was sure: loss of his job, excommunication, and a life very different than what he had envisioned.[3] Perhaps more than anything else, his own partial embrace of the martyr narrative shows its persuasive power, explaining his life experiences as part of a broader and meaningful sacrifice for faith and for truth.

Most recently, the martyr narrative can be heard in Benjamin Park's 2022 podcast interview on RadioWest. In it, Park notes that

---

2. Lavina Fielding Anderson, "DNA Mormon: D. Michael Quinn" in *Mormon Mavericks: Essays on Dissenters*, ed. John Sillito and Susan Staker (Salt Lake City, UT: Signature Books, 2002), 329–63.

3. See Gary Topping, *D. Michael Quinn: Mormon Historian* (Salt Lake City: Signature Books, 2022), 108–09.

to some Quinn is a hero, a martyr figure, and a "person who fought against the institution trying to preserve the validity of true investigation, of unbiased analysis."[4] Here we see that the martyr narrative is alluring precisely because of its simplicity and its romance. It is about someone who sacrifices, often their entire life to die either a social or a physical death for the truth. In addition to its declaration that the truth will eventually win out, the martyr story allows communities to assert that the death of the martyr is *meaningful*.[5] In Quinn's case, we see the meaning tied to concepts of truth and how the truth does not always upend faith but can deepen it. The martyr narrative suggests that the social or physical death of the martyr is somehow "worth it" because it is a sacrifice for the greater good of the community's values—in this case, those of liberal progressive Mormons and, to some degree, Mormon studies scholars.

Yet the martyr story has its problems, and this is something that Quinn himself also rightfully acknowledged. When he spoke of the persecution early Mormon church members faced, he said, "As appealing as the martyr [story] is for anyone who has been picked on at a personal level or any group historically, usually it is more complex than that."[6] Although in the RadioWest interview Park stands apart from the martyrization of Quinn, recognizing and reflecting on the appeal of the narrative, he also partakes in its telling: "What is tragic is while he might have … been living alone, he is seen as a beloved figure by tens of thousands of academics, of Mormons, of the marginalized. As a pioneer of LGBTQ history. As someone who is willing to speak truth to power."[7] In just a few sentences, Park hales Quinn as a *pioneer*, which carries substantial weight for a primarily Latter-day Saint audience and he emphasizes his importance to so many people. Yet in the same sentence, Park mentions that Quinn was living alone when he died. Why might that be a part of the story

4. Benjamin E. Park, "The Life and Legacy of Michael Quinn," interview by Doug Fabrizio, *RadioWest*, Feb. 24, 2022, radiowest.kuer.org.

5. Elizabeth A. Castelli, *Martyrdom and Memory: Early Christian Culture Making* (New York: Columbia University Press, 2007), 2–5. See also Sara M. Patterson, *Pioneers in the Attic: Place and Memory along the Mormon Trail* (New York: Oxford University Press, 2020), 141–44.

6. D. Michael Quinn, "21st Century Mormon Enigma," interview with John Dehlin, *Mormon Stories* podcast, episodes 285–287, Sep. 17, 2011, mormonstories.org.

7. Park, "Life and Legacy."

as it is so often recounted? Sure, it captures the social death aspect of the martyr story, but I think there is more here. Why does Quinn's aloneness matter in our tellings of his life?

Let's hold onto to that question as we move to the second narrative.

This next rendering has locked Quinn into a linear trajectory that begins with his life as a rising star in church history. He was recognized for his intellect, married to a beautiful wife, teaching at Brigham Young University, and creating a family. His was the life that LDS theology and its social hierarchies dictate as *the best*. This LDS narrative of progression toward exaltation—I will call it the exaltative narrative—is intertwined with the capitalistic, future-oriented, heterosexual, production model of time of the broader culture. Together these religious and cultural narratives rest on three pillars: production, reproduction, and exaltation.[8] They emphasize the importance of the "Child" imagined as symbolic of the future's "unquestioned value" and "meaning's eventual realization."[9] This "Child" serves as both the goad and the goal for activity within this life; it is imagined as the inheritor of all of the productivity and reproductivity in which humans take part.

LDS theology takes the broader cultural narratives of production and reproduction even one step further with the Plan of Salvation. In this framework, the pre-mortal spirit develops into the mortal and eventually the post-mortal realm where, because of one's effort, both in terms of production and reproduction, the individual is rewarded for the labor that they have accomplished—the reward is exaltation. It is a theological system that connects the individual to the past as the inheritors of morals and values and looks ahead to the future familial connections that will come to full fruition for time and eternity.[10]

While this narrative is prevalent in virtually every account of his life, it surfaces even in the most recent retelling of Quinn's life, Gary

8. J. Jack Halberstam describes it as "family, heterosexuality, and reproduction" in *In a Queer Time and Place: Transgender Bodies, Subcultural Lives* (New York: New York University Press, 2005), 1–2.

9. Lee Edelman, *No Future: Queer Theory and the Death Drive* (Durham, NC: Duke University Press, 2004), 3–4. See also Elizabeth Freeman, *Time Binds: Queer Temporalities, Queer Histories* (Durham, NC: Duke University Press, 2010).

10. See Halberstam, *In a Queer Time and Place*, 5–6. See also Patterson, *Pioneers in the Attic*.

Topping's biography titled *D. Michael Quinn*. Roughly 80% of the book focuses on the linear rise of Quinn in his scholarship, family life, and career. Quinn's tipping point comes with his recognition that he could no longer live a lie in terms of his sexuality, his colleagues' harassment of him, his loss of access to his temple recommend, and his "realization that martyrdom, both academic and ecclesiastical, probably awaited him."[11] A brief dozen or so pages follows Quinn's excommunication, even though he lived almost another thirty years. Although Topping describes Quinn's life during that time as "an incongruous mixture of productivity and drift," recognizing his scholarly productivity after his excommunication, the book also discusses the financial problems that "dogged him constantly." (His scholarly productivity did not bring him the financial means to support himself the way his initial career path would have.) Topping further relates the fact that Quinn "was alone in his condominium when he died from a heart attack."[12] There are two underlying messages in this framing. First, Quinn's financial instability is noted as part of his linear descent: he could no longer be productive in the ways he had previously been. And second, his family all but disappears from the narratives of his life, even though we know that he maintained a friendship with his ex-wife and relationships with his children.

Finally, Topping adds that "Quinn had always lived on the edge, personally, intellectually and ecclesiastically, and thus he had always been, in a sense, alone." This left Topping to "wonder if there was perhaps something fitting in the fact that he died as he had lived."[13] And so we have a narrative of linear rise followed by linear descent, and again, and perhaps most intriguingly, we have a narrative where once he is in his linear fall, the emphasis is placed on Quinn being *alone*. Here, the martyr narrative reinforces the productive-reproductive-exaltative narrative: in order to achieve "the truth," Quinn sacrificed all of his connections.

Perhaps most problematically, that narrative also suggests that living into his true self in terms of his sexuality cost him all of his relationships. While it is clear that coming out had its costs, including

---

11. Topping, *D. Michael Quinn*, 98–111.
12. Topping, 120, 122, 123.
13. Topping, 123.

pain for his wife and other family members, that simply did not
end his familial ties. Quinn's aloneness in these narratives is serving an entirely different function. It operates as both a warning, a
cautionary tale, but also a celebration of a martyr sacrificing all for a
bigger cause. In accepting the emphasis on Quinn's aloneness, we accept the narrative of the culture and religion that found Quinn's life
wanting—one that had relegated him to a place outside the bounds
of acceptable time.

And so Mike Quinn has been locked into heteroproductive, reproductive, and exaltative linear understandings of time and futurity.
His aloneness at the end of his life signals his failure to fulfill the
cultural and religious narratives placed upon him.

It is the concept of queer time, however, that we can use to liberate
him and see him anew outside of the bounds of how he has been narrated in the past. Queer time upsets the linear notion of time in which
we are "enjoined to make all our own pleasures and commitments
secondary to a future that never comes [and that] does not privilege
the future at the expense of the present and past."[14] In the words of
queer theorist Jack Halberstam, queer time is about the unexpected,
refusing to live a life scripted by the markers deemed necessary by the
broader culture, "namely, birth, marriage, reproduction, and death,"
and, I would add for LDS narratives, exaltation.[15] Queer time em-
braces the present, the partial, and the enjoyment of the momentary,
stepping out of the linear and future-oriented narratives that surround
us. It disrupts the understanding of meaning taken from a heteroreproductive model and denies the teleological, the *straight*jacket
of meaning placed on modern understandings of time.[16] Queering
time does not mean that members of the LGBTQ community do not
want children or a future that cares for those children, but it serves
instead as a metaphorical disruption of the imposition of meaning
onto life vis-à-vis a future that is always just out of one's grasp.[17] In
Quinn's case, embracing queer time meant rejecting the narratives

14. Elena Levy-Navarro, "Fattening Queer History," in Esther Rothblum and Sondra
Solovay, eds. *The Fat Studies Reader* (New York: New York University Press, 2009), 15–22.

15. Halberstam, *In a Queer Time and Place*, 2.

16. Edelman, *No Future*, 27. Edelman writes that Queer time rejects the "spiritual-
ization through marriage to reproductive futurism."

17. Edelman, *No Future*, 13, 17–18.

of the church that put him in a lock-step march toward career, the nuclear family, and the promise of the next life.

While I cannot briefly explore all the ways that queering time might enable us to see Quinn's life in new ways, I want to hold up two moments in his life in which we might see the value of liberating Quinn from these problematic narratives we have so often told about him. Scholars have related them so frequently that we've come to believe they make up *the narrative of his life*, a life which peaked too early and then descended into disintegration, drift, meandering, and meaninglessness. The two moments share one thing in common: they both happened when the church was holding disciplinary councils against Quinn.

The first episode, in July of 1993, was when Quinn was disfellowshipped. It came after a series of interactions with Paul Hanks, his stake president, who had identified both Quinn's scholarship and his homosexuality as the reasons for his hearing. Quinn's response was moving and firm and pushed back against the narratives being told about him: "I sincerely hope you never are in the situation of being hunted down by those you regard as prophets, seers, and revelators, but who have defined you as expendable."[18] In an interesting interplay, Quinn accepted and affirmed the sacred roles of the church leadership and yet understood that he stood outside their understandings of time and value. He was expendable precisely because he no longer fit into their narratives of productivity, reproductivity, and exaltation.

That first council determined that he would no longer be received as a full member in one of his primary social networks. This decision was simply an extension of the initial loss of his temple recommend and therefore his access to the temple, the place where he could enact the rituals of his faith that reinforced the larger narratives of the theological worldview supported by the church.[19] Quinn was placed further and further outside of church constructions of time, his future now a big question mark. His divorce and disciplinary councils rendered him an outsider to the heteroreproductive theology that

---

18. Quoted in Anderson, "DNA Mormon," 350.

19. For a discussion of the loss of his temple recommend, see Topping, *D. Michael Quinn*, 111.

the church teaches and taught. Yet, as his fellow church members met to determine his standing, Quinn decided not to engage in the process of the disciplinary council. Instead he chose to go see the movie *Super Mario Brothers*.[20] He chose the present moment, and a film about a meteorite crashing into the earth and splitting the universe into two dimensions, one with a race of human-like creatures descended from dinosaurs, to participating in the dissolution of his ties to his social and faith networks and the life narratives he had been taught to value. It was after that movie that he reported feeling a sense of calm coming over him.[21] He had chosen queer time to the church hierarchy's constructions of time and his place in it.

Not two months later, Quinn again refused to take part in another disciplinary council, this one held on September 26, 1993. Quinn was not in Utah at the time. Instead, he had chosen to go to California to attend and present at the Affirmation conference (a group of LGBTQ+ Mormons).[22] Rather than participating in a process that would sever his connection to church community and institutional authority, Quinn traveled outside the bounds of orthodoxy both literally and metaphorically and entered into the community of Affirmation. Their archived newsletters affirm Mike Quinn as a superstar at Affirmation conferences, along with John Boswell, author of *Christianity, Social Tolerance and Homosexuality*, a book that discusses homosexuality in Christian history.[23] Quinn is, of course, mentioned with his monumental book, *Same-Sex Dynamics in Nineteenth-Century Americans: A Mormon Example*.[24]

What is clear in the Affirmation newsletters is the importance of that book to the Affirmation community. It provided them with a sense of a usable past, the ability to see that the queer Mormon

---

20. David Haglund, "The Case of the Mormon Historian," *Slate*, Nov. 2012, 12. Quinn was disfellowshipped at this council, an act that meant "placing him on probation, denying him the sacraments and exercise of his priesthood ministry, and even denying him the right to give his testimony in church." See Topping, *D. Michael Quinn*, 119.

21. Anderson, "DNA Mormon," 352.

22. Haglund, "Case of the Mormon Historian," 13. In addition to attending the affirmation conference, Quinn stayed in California for several days.

23. John Boswell, *Christianity, Social Tolerance and Homosexuality* (Chicago: University of Chicago Press, 1981).

24. D. Michael Quinn, *Same-Sex Dynamics among Nineteenth-Century Americans: A Mormon Example* (Urbana: University of Illinois Press, 2001).

community stretched back in time and had survived the long haul.[25] Take, for example, the book review written by John Gustav-Wrathall, future president and executive director of Affirmation. Gustav-Wrathall knew the impact of church policies and teachings about homosexuality all too well. He had been haunted by the words of Boyd K. Packer as he contemplated death by suicide in his youth, believing "that, as a gay man, my life had no value."[26] Here Gustav-Wrathall framed his life in terms of value, recognizing that his queer life did not live up to the productive-reproductive-exaltative narrative expectations of the church. Reading Quinn's book helped him see the world differently: "[Quinn's] portrait of 'the world we have lost' is compelling and moving, even as it poses larger questions about the world we have gained."[27] Members of Affirmation created a new sense of family structure and inheritance, offering alternative histories to the stories told in LDS cultures. They found and lifted up their own pioneers. Of course, they hoped that the presence of earlier tolerance within the church's history might indicate the coming of a hoped-for future of greater acceptance in the LDS community; but more importantly, they created community in moments and places that stood outside the reach of the narratives of the LDS Church.

In these two moments—where Quinn disregarded the church's attempt to impose meaning and narratives on his life and chose instead to step outside of church concepts of time—Quinn created his own peace in queer time. He created and embraced a new community and a new family structure with its own understandings of time, inheritance, and the future. In so doing, he challenged the narrative impositions that so many have placed on him. The constant reference to his living and dying alone in those imposing narratives that saw his life in a linear descent need reframing. The concept of queer time—of perhaps only brief but most importantly disruptive moments—can help us better think about Quinn's life.

---

25. See Alexandria Griffin, "Queer Mormon Histories and the Politics of a Usable Past," *Dialogue: A Journal of Mormon Thought* 54, no. 1 (Spring 2021): 5–9 for a discussion of the past serving as a framework for a possible future where LGBTQ+ folk are welcomed in the church.

26. John D. Gustav-Wrathall, review of *Same-Sex Dynamics among Nineteenth Century Americans: A Mormon Example, Journal of Mormon History* 32, no. 1 (Spring 2006), 260.

27. Gustav-Wrathall.

Quinn was a historian who looked to the past for answers to questions about faith, but he was also a man who had learned how to live a solitary life. After resigning from BYU and winning the Mormon History Association's (MHA) best book award, he wrote that he "traveled in a solitary manner, even when in [MHA members'] company," and that he "was beginning a 'separate peace.' With myself, with my sense of mission, with God."[28] Years later he described himself as a Mormon mystic, saying, "It's you and me God."[29] So while Quinn continued his quest for the truth, he chose to create new understandings of family, community, and faith. He continued his relationship with his God. He continued to have moments of queer time. And he certainly created meaning long after September 1993 in ways that have been overlooked and made invisible by the imposition of the straightjacket of heteroreproductive, productive, and exaltative linear time.

---

28. Quotation from 1988 memoir found in Joseph W. Geisner, ed., "On Writing Mormon History, 1972–95, from the Diaries and Memoirs of D. Michael Quinn," in Joseph W. Geisner, ed., *Writing Mormon History: Historians and Their Books* (Salt Lake City: Signature Books, 2020), 269–70.

29. Quoted in Park, "Life and Legacy." Similarly, in his Mormon Stories interview he referred to himself as "a church of one."

Michael Peña Quinn: A Chicano with Gringo Attitude and Experience[1]

SUJEY VEGA

Though Peña is not a name most would associate with D. Michael Quinn, it was his father's actual original surname. Though Quinn never used Peña himself, centering this surname marks my attempt to help rescue his Mexican lineage. As a Gender Studies professor, I make it a point not to use a person's dead name. A dead name, or the name assigned to a trans/queer person at birth, represents a time when someone's full self and gender identity went denied. As Chakravarty and English note in their work on LGBTQ populations in Utah, "Calling people by their preferred name, pronouns, and chosen identity label is a way to affirm people's humanity."[2] Using a dead name can, and often does, get weaponized by those who insist on rejecting someone's true gender identity or expression.[3] To use someone's dead name is a cruel and homophobic act, akin to a slur.

---

1. I want to thank the Quinn family and Jan for taking the time to talk to me and provide any insight into Mike's enigmatic family history. I also want to express my appreciation to Sara Patterson for bringing Quinn's 2000 Sunstone letter to my attention.

2. Debjani Chakravarty and Monica English, "'I Don't Like Going To Gay Pride': Experiences of Negotiating LGBTQIA Mormon Identity in Utah," *Sexuality & Culture* 25, no. 1 (2020): 235–54.

3. This can also be termed misgendering. For more readings on misgendering, dead names or the impact of this types of microaggressionst, see, in addition to Chakravarty and English, Jacqui Gabb, Elizabeth McDermott, Rachael Eastham, and Ali Hanbury, "Paradoxical Family Practices: LGBTQ+ Young People, Mental Health and Wellbeing," *Journal of Sociology (Melbourne, Vic.)* 56, no. 4 (2020): 535–53; Edward F. Lomash, Tabria D. Brown, and M. Paz Galupo, "'A Whole Bunch of Love the Sinner Hate the Sin': LGBTQ Microaggressions Experienced in Religious and Spiritual Context," *Journal of Homosexuality* 66, no. 10 (2019): 1495–1511; Annie Pullen Sansfaçon et al., "Parents' Journeys to Acceptance and Support of Gender-Diverse and Trans Children and Youth," *Journal of Family Issues* 41, no. 8 (2020): 1214–36.

I begin with this explanation as a means to clarify that Peña is not a dead name. For Quinn, Peña was a name denied to him by his father.

Clearly, gender identity/expression and white passing are two distinct experiences.[4] One affirms identity, the other denies it. White passing, as Jason Palmer identifies with Peruvian LDS members, refers to "a white Latino who can pass as completely Anglo."[5] Deeply embedded in the LDS Church's own dysfunctional history with racism, this colorism affords some privileges to white passing Latinos both in the church and in the United States as a whole.[6] As a result, Quinn's life, and that of his Mexican American father are intertwined with stories of denial, rejection, queerness, and closeted identities. This chapter provides Quinn's family, and those who grew up mixed-race like him, some inspiration to dig deeper into their cultural heritage. By focusing on the Peña side of Quinn's story, I hope to illustrate how the pain and repudiation of the father carried over to the son.

Quinn admitted later in his life that he "would prefer to live anywhere except Latin America. Despite being Chicano, I'm a Gringo in attitude and experience." Importantly, even during his years of underemployed wandering, he did not explicitly desire to visit Mexico. And yet in 1999 he decided to visit Chiapas, Mexico, an ancestral home. And he documented his trip in a revealing diary.

But before understanding this revealing trip, and the journal that documented it, one must understand Quinn's familial history.

Daniel Peña, aka Donald Quinn

To understand the son, I had to try to understand the father. What would lead a Mexican American man to cut off his identity, change his name, and close off that part of him to his children? What could have occurred for Daniel Peña to deny his family and put on the skin of "Donald Quinn"? Why deny his own mother,

---

4. Although Chakravarty and English, "Gay Pride," present a compelling case of how in Utah asexual and cis-gendered (folks who identify with their gender at birth) can experience "passing privileges—in a way queer and transgender individuals cannot" (249).

5. Jason Charles Palmer, "Barriers to Sainthood: Mormon Families, Times, and Places Between Peru and Utah," PhD diss., University of California Irvine, 2021, 161.

6. Jane Lilly Lopez et al., "Shades of Belonging: The Intersection of Race and Religion in Utah Immigrants' Social Integration." *Social Sciences (Basel)* 10, no. 246 (2021): 246–.

Carmela Peña, and his siblings from being a part of his life? And more to the point, how did this deception affect his descendants, including Michael? Whatever trauma Donald experienced echoed and reverberated onto Michael's own suppressed negative associations with Mexico. This rupture in identity and family trauma filtered not just into the historian's life, but also into his children, grandchildren, nieces, and nephews who now find themselves struggling with how they connect or continue to sever their Mexican lineage.

Donald, Michael's father, died long ago and without answering the above questions. All we have are puzzle pieces that help us contextualize his experience as a Mexican American in East Los Angeles. Through some historical background on the area and experience of Mexican Americans at the time, perhaps we can better understand why Daniel Peña would try his hand at white passing. Michael came of age in the 1960s, during the Chicano Civil Rights Era and in a moment when the LDS Church was trying to carefully navigate questions of race and ethnicity. Unraveling the historical moments taking shape during the lives of both Donald and Michael provides a snapshot, though incomplete, of how these men came to see themselves in response to or in spite of this timeline in Mexican American history.

Donald Quinn was born Daniel Peña in Arizona to Mexican immigrant parents in 1912. The family moved to East Los Angeles in the area just northwest of the contemporary tourist destination of Olvera Street [Image from digital archives- Huntington Library]. Given Peña's Arizona connections, it is very possible that his family settled near Sonoratown, because it was the only place Mexican were allowed to live at that time. Sonoratown, like Chinatown, came about as a result of segregation and prejudice. Adobe houses, packed dirt floors, and the dominance of Spanish came to define Los Angeles' first barrio. Importantly, barrio here does not mean ward as is traditionally translated in the LDS Church. This reference to barrio is "a zone of segregation and repression" and additionally "el barrio is the reaffirmation of culture, a defense of space, an ethnically bounded sanctuary, and the spiritual zone of Chicana/o and Mexicana/o identity."[7] As a site of refuge and oppression, barrios

7. David R. Diaz, *Barrio Urbanism: Chicanos, Planning and American Cities* (London: Routledge, 2005), 3.

can be enriching and debilitating at the same time. For some, like Donald, segregated barrios like Sonoratown in Los Angeles came to represent a place of great shame.

Confined to this area of town, it is very likely the Peña family struggled to eke out a living. Indeed, Daniel's childhood friend, actor Anthony Quinn, wrote to Mike once explaining that Daniel was the eldest of his siblings and often the wage earner for the entire Peña family. This information confirms what Michael's family speculates as a source of conflict with the elder Peña, or Daniel's father. Though murky, it is believed some sort of conflict between Daniel and his father led to a familial rupture. As a young boy, Daniel even asked Anthony Quinn's family to adopt him into their family.

Long before Anthony Quinn would grace the screens of Hollywood's golden age, Dan and Anthony became good friends in this barrio [insert map]. Indeed, it was seeing Dan act in his school productions that gave Anthony Quinn the encouragement to try his own hand in the business.[8] They were such good friends that Dan wished desperately to be a part of the Quinn family instead of his own. Given their own humble beginnings, however, the Quinns could not adopt Dan. Sometime later, the two boys had a falling out, perhaps in their late teens. Once they went their separate ways, Dan decided to develop a character, a persona, that he named Donald Quinn. In spite of not being adopted by them, Dan informally appropriated Quinn as his last name and later changed from Daniel to Donald. So began his journey to fully disconnect himself from his family and his heritage.

Perhaps it was a combination of conflicts with Dan's father and the societal racism he surely faced that led to his identity break. He came of age in Los Angeles during the Deportation/Repatriation raids of the 1930s.[9] The anti-Mexican sentiment prevalent at the time led Dan to deny his family in order to save himself. As Michael

8. From private correspondence from Anthony Quinn to Mike Quinn, in D. Michael Quinn, "Journal/Journey of a Gringo Chicano in Mexico," unpublished manuscript in my possession.

9. For more on Mexican repatriations, see Francisco E. Balderrama and Raymond Rodriguez, *Decade of Betrayal: Mexican Repatriation in the 1930s*, rev. ed. (Albuquerque: University of New Mexico Press, 2006); David Carrasco, *Religions of Mesoamerica*, 2nd ed. (Long Grove, IL: Waveland Press, 2013).

Women in front of an adobe in Sonoratown, east side of Sunset. *Courtesy of The Hutington Library, San Marino, California.*

Quinn once remarked about his father, "as a teenager, 'white' boys called him 'spic' and 'wetback.' He vowed to escape from being loathed by the vast majority and from the poverty he thought typical of his own people."[10] By 1943, the year before Mike Quinn was born, this anti-Mexican antagonism intensified and resulted in the violence against Mexican Americans during the Zoot Suit Riots.[11] Amidst national war efforts and rationing of clothing material, agitated servicemen targeted young Mexican American youth and went on a violent rampage, attacking them with impunity from the police.

When Michael was born in 1944, Donald continued the big lie. Indeed, Michael's mother only knew about Donald's true background after they were married when he drove his wife to the working-poor neighborhood he grew up in. He pulled up to his mother's home and told his wife at that moment that this was where he was raised. She

10. D. Michael Quinn, "Ever-GR..." *Sunstone*, Feb. 2000, 6–7.

11. For more on the Zoot Suit Riots, see Eduardo Obregón Pagán, *Murder at the Sleepy Lagoon: Zoot Suits, Race, and Riot in Wartime L.A.* (Chapel Hill: The University of North Carolina Press, 2003), and Catherine Sue Ramírez, *The Woman in the Zoot Suit: Gender, Nationalism, and the Cultural Politics of Memory* (Durham: Duke University Press, 2009).

briefly met Carmelita Peña, Donald's mother, who greeted Mike's mother with an ominous message: "I feel so sorry for you."[12]

Quinn's Chicano Identity

It is unclear when exactly Michael Quinn found out about his father's actual identity. It was likely around the time that the Chicano Civil Rights Movement (1965–75) was well underway.[13] Jan, his wife at the time, recounts that he was never ashamed to be part Mexican, but he never felt he could fully claim it as an identity given that he lived his whole life as a white man.

When Quinn was an active member of the LDS Church, he must have been aware of active discussions within Mormonism on the meaning and making of a Chicano Mormon Identity.[14] University of Utah professor Orlando Rivera pointed out in 1978 that there was an underlying superiority complex feeding into the way white Mormons viewed Latinos as linguistically, culturally, and intellectually deficient.[15] It is unclear if Quinn ever heard of Rivera or his interventions on Chicano Mormonism, or how and if Mike interacted with Ignacio Garcia from BYU's History Department. Both Rivera and Garcia were scholars in Mike's reach who openly explored Chicano History, identity, and Mormonism. Yet, he himself seemed not to participate in this discussion of Chicano identity.

While Quinn was always aware of his genealogical ties to Mexico, he never equated his lineage with identity. Quinn eventually did speak to his half-sisters (from his father's second marriage) and heard about an uncle Jimmy, Daniel's brother. Beyond finding some genealogical ties to a fishing town near the Gulf of Mexico, however,

---

12. Gary Topping, *D. Michael Quinn: Mormon Historian* (Salt Lake City: Signature Books, 2022), 2.

13. For more on the Chicana/o Civil Rights Movement, see Mario T García, *Mexican Americans: Leadership, Ideology & Identity, 1930–1960* (New Haven: Yale University Press, 1989); Ignacio M Garcia, *Chicano While Mormon: Activism, War, and Keeping the Faith* (Cranbury: The Rowman & Littlefield Publishing Group, 2015); Maylei Blackwell, ¡Chicana Power! Contested Histories of Feminism in the Chicano Movement (Austin: University of Texas Press, 2011); Lee Bebout, *Mythohistorical Interventions the Chicano Movement and Its Legacies* (Minneapolis: University of Minnesota Press, 2011).

14. For a deeper exploration of Chicano and Mormon identity, see Garcia, *Chicano While Mormon*.

15. Orlando Rivera, "Mormonism and the Chicano," in *Mormonism: A Faith for All Cultures*, ed. F. LaMond Tullis (Provo, UT: Brigham Young University Press, 1978), 115–26.

it seems that Quinn never delved deeper into his actual Chicano or, to be more precise, his Mexican American past. What we do know from his journals is that Mike demonstrates a perhaps un-conscious distance or rather distaste for Mexico that his father laid the groundwork for. Importantly, his brief time in Mexico also came as Mike was battling depression and struggling to define himself in this new life as an unpaid full-time researcher/writer.

An Unexpected, and Unrewarding, Pilgrimage

When Michael Quinn visited Chiapas from February 1999 to July 1999, it was far from a pleasure trip to the land of his ancestors. Exiled without steady income and with credit debt piling up, his time in Chiapas was merely a stopgap until he could get back on his feet. Quinn's "gringo attitude" may have manifested in the way he resisted the people and culture of Mexico. As I read his journal, I picked up on an underlined, yet palpable, distaste for Mexico. To say that Quinn enjoyed his time in Mexico would be a stretch. Moshe, his son, confirmed as much and explained how his father had a com-plex relationship with his heritage.

Michael Quinn, unlike his father, never hid the fact that he was part Mexican. From the moment he was made aware of his father's true name (Daniel Peña), he acknowledged his genetic ties to Mex-ico. Quinn even adapted the language of the time and self-identified as a "Chicano." This juxtaposition between identifying as Chicano while exhibiting an aversion to the actual culture, food, bureaucracy, and toxic masculinity (or machismo), however, is problematic. To be Chicano also means being politically engaged or, in today's parlance, decolonizing oneself from Anglo and Spanish hegemony while re-cuperating indigenous identity.[16] Rather than lean into his heritage and find ways to rescue this past to reconcile the present, Quinn's short time spent in Mexico only served to confirm why his father wanted to distance himself from his ethnicity.

Between the homophobia he experienced and the cultural detach-ment his father created, Quinn did not grow to love the land erased

---

16. For a good summary of Chicano identity in the 1970s, see Gustavo V. Segade, "Identity and Power: An Essay on the Politics of Culture and the Culture of Politics in Chicano Thought," *Aztlán* 9, no. 1 (1978): 85–99.

from his identity. Grateful for his friend's hacienda that served as a reprieve from the financial strains back in the United States, he expressed frustrations and dissatisfaction from his paternal culture. Hence, he wished "to live anywhere except Latin America." Indeed, though Quinn had experience living in other regions of the world— Germany for instance—it was the entirety of Latin American that repelled him. This disdain for Latin America was the collective result of having all ties to this identity denied to him, unconsciously adopting Eurocentric ideals and white privilege related to the LDS Church, and encountering homophobic slights while in Chiapas.

After initially reading some of Mike's journal and the relevant chapter from Gary Topping's biography, I felt unsettled about how I could analyze this plagued journey between self, lineage, identity, and shame. Many Mexican Americans feel a kind of culture shock when we first arrive in Mexico. One is unsure of their own cultural competency in the real Mexico, and one's accented Spanish becomes almost paralyzing. Many of us in this identity limbo feel the classic Chicano proverb of being "not Mexican enough for Mexico and not American enough for America." Our own hang-ups and insecurities bubble to the surface the minute our authenticity is called into question by Mexican nationals.

Quinn felt this culture shock, but in a skewed way. His Americanness and white privilege was never questioned, but here, in the land where his grandparents lived, he felt no connection. Rather than learn to embrace this side of his heritage, or have what religious studies scholar David Carrasco[17] described as an "Aztec moment" (albeit in Chiapas), Quinn's gringo attitude was very present when speaking of machismo, homophobia, diarrhea, and his overall contempt for the culture and bureaucracy of Mexico. I mean, he boiled bottles of purified water for god's sake.

Though Utah certainly exhibited its own toxic masculinity and homophobia, his critique of Mexico's patriarchy somehow felt more pointed and judgmental. Like in the U.S., Latina women and men struggle with defining themselves against a gender binary and expectations attributed to gender roles. Masculinity plagues many

17. Carrasco, *Religions of Mesoamerica*, describes a visit to the Templo Mayor museum in Mexico City when he felt cosmically connected to an ancestral spirituality.

a society. Rather than play into tired racist stereotypes that label "machismo" as a Latin American problem, the better question asks how expectations of manhood result in violence, homophobia, and patriarchy even in the Global North. Moreover, taking an intersectional framing within Mormonism allows us to situate how gender expectations operate through the context of national, cultural, raced, classed, and religious environments.[18] In this manner, one can see the potential overlaps and differences between toxic masculinity in Utah and in Mexico. Regretfully, Quinn's journals did not reveal such nuanced engagement. Instead, his reflections reveal how he struggled with his "Gringo attitude" in as much as he praised the German language and living in Europe. Indeed, he even sought Swiss citizenship because his mother's grandmother was from Bern.

In spite of his clear preference for Europe over Latin America, Quinn stayed in luxury in a nice Hacienda surrounded by the culture and people that were denied to him as a child. And yet he still resisted. In those weeks, he expressed what best can be described as shame for not knowing the language and customs of his supposed heritage. Without a positive Mexican role model to train him up in his ethnicity, and perhaps his own father's lifelong goal to distance himself from all things Mexican, these cultural barriers may have actually seeped into Mike's own subconscious.

It was painful for me, a Chicana who was raised to appreciate her Mexican heritage, to read what a difficult time Quinn had while in Mexico. While there were moments of convivial exchange with locals, the journal kept returning to the stage that we in anthropology would call "culture shock." The shock is not so much related to surprise, but to resistance of the unknown. Refusal to experience the lives and customs of others feeds our own fears that we simply do not belong or are unfamiliar with a specific cultural experience. So, we keep people, foods, and cultural experiences as arm's length as we interpret what we see through the lens of antipathy. This is, I feel, is what Quinn struggled with. His own insecurities, his lack

---

18. For more on intersectionality and LDS experiences, see Sujey Vega, "Intersectional Hermanas: LDS Latinas Navigate Faith, Leadership and Sisterhood," *Latino Studies* 17, no. 1 (2019): 27–47.

of Spanish linguistic skills, his father's ethnic suppression, and his hyper-awareness of homophobic snubs all distorted how Mike would take in Mexico.

Ethnicity and Sexuality

Quinn's discomfort with Mexican culture can be best seen in the way he writes about being queer in rural Mexico's heteronormative space. As noted earlier, homophobic antipathy was equally present in Utah and other spaces of the United States. Quinn therefore almost expected homophobia in Chiapas as it was tied to his ideas of machismo. Indeed, it took him five months in Mexico to realize that "Mexican homophobia is not consistent," and that some aspects of male to male affection were widely acceptable, even among straight men.[19] Quinn struggled to find a lover, or at least someone with whom he could connect, while in Mexico. His search for companionship was present throughout his journal. Even in this space, a culture and people he was far from familiar with, he hungered for a relationship, a partnership, or even a quick affair that would ease the absence of connection he felt with his surroundings.

Quinn wrote a letter in the Opinion section *Sunstone* (Yea Yea/Nay Nay section) while he was in Chiapas and though he references ethnicity and culture, the piece reveals how he was engrossed in thinking about sexual identity. In the letter there is very little reference to Quinn's own ties to Mexico or connecting in any way with the culture (beyond a reference to eating burritos). Instead, Quinn imagines an "'ethnic reorientation' support-group" and contemplates the ridiculousness of rejecting one's true ethnicity through the tropes used in homophobic "conversion" therapy. He ends by arguing for a "divine kingdom where any of us would be happy to dwell with others who are really 'our kind.'"[20] I wonder what Quinn meant by "our kind," given the focus of the piece he was certainly speaking of ethnicity through the lens of sexuality. This moment speaks to Quinn's frustrations with what he perceived as Mexico's lack of queer affirming spaces. Perhaps he himself may not have been conscious of this connection, but I perceive this *Sunstone* letter as indicative of

19. Quinn, "Journal/Journey."
20. D. Michael Quinn, "Ever-GR…," 6–7.

Quinn's own conflict with identifying with Mexico. Centering his sexuality left little room to connect to other aspects of himself or even explore intersectional framings of being both Mexican and gay.

Quinn struggled to find a thriving queer community in Chiapas and was unsure of himself when interacting with potential queer partners. The fear of misreading a situation, missing the social cues, and being rejected for his age was, I feel, indicative of larger concerns for feeling out of place and out of sorts in Mexico. Regretfully, Quinn did not return to Mexico and missed the chance to see the active and thriving Queer Mexican community that may have helped ease his deficiency in cultural and sexual encounters. In fact, not far from Chiapas are the Zapotec communities of Oaxaca who are recognized as Muxe, or gender non-confirming individuals, we might call them trans in the United States. Here the Muxe navigate both traditional Mexican culture while pushing the boundaries of gender expression and gender identity.

Though Quinn may not have directly identified with their gender-bending identities, he would have benefiting from knowing about this long-established queer community in the Zapotec communities just West of Chiapas. I wish Quinn would have given Mexico an opportunity to prove itself as a place, culture, and people worthy of his identity. In rescuing that part of him that his father rejected, Michael Quinn could have broadened his life and opened his heart to the possibilities of love and passion in Mexico. Alas, he passed before he was able to give his patrilineage a second chance.

Michael Quinn as a Dissenter in Mormon History

MAXINE HANKS

When one considers D. Michael Quinn's work on Mormon history, the first thing that comes to mind is his dissenting perspective, which transcended existing discourse with new original research and uncommon insights that dismantled standard views and the status quo. "Dissent" means to disagree, differ with, or depart from views previously, commonly, or officially held. Quinn's scholarship offered dissenting views on Mormon history for fifty years, from 1972 until his death in 2021. He was also a dissenting figure himself in that period of time, a human symbol of the costs of dissent within a religious culture.

However, more than merely dissenting, Mike Quinn was "deconstructive": he aimed to undo the underlying structures of dominant discourses, showing how they disempower or distort reality, history and its participants, by revealing what they privilege and what they subvert, then reversing those terms to recover the subverted. Quinn deconstructed privilege, hegemony, and marginalization of the "Other" on every topic he engaged. His work consistently gave the subverted "Other" its due attention and validity, as a partner of privilege within a larger dynamic that includes both. Quinn saw truth on all sides, in all voices and their positions, and explored them from the inside with empathy for each on its own terms. The "D." in D. Michael Quinn could have stood for "deconstructive"—as his major works reveal.

In September 1981, Mike gave a landmark lecture to the BYU Student History Association titled "On Being a Mormon Historian" that directly refuted a BYU speech by LDS Apostle Boyd K. Packer in August 1981, "The Mantle is Far, Far Greater than the Intellect." In his address, Elder Packer instructed Mormon historians at BYU to place loyalty to the church and its leaders over scholarly investigations and critiques of the church. He advised scholars not to "judge the Church ... by the principles of their own profession ... [but] judge the professions of man by the revealed word of the Lord." Packer further urged scholars to show "the workings of God ... in every hour and in every moment ... of the Church, from its beginning until now" rather than "the weaknesses and frailties" which "destroys faith" adding that "in the Church we are not neutral. We are one-sided."[1]

Quinn rejected these premises due to their privileging of faith over intellect, and loyalty over critique. He indicted such advice as advocating a "Mormon History ... [that] would border on idolatry" rather than value honesty. He saw the belief that prophets only express the will of God as the "Mormon equivalent of...papal infallibility." A "prophet who is incapable of ... error," he argued, "has no free agency." Quinn saw a false dichotomy in pitting faith against scholarship which "created an enemy that does not exist." He preferred a "sacred history" as in the Bible and Book of Mormon where the prophets are human, flawed, imperfect.[2]

This was a rare act of public dissent by a BYU professor against a church leader. Privately, some scholars quipped that "The mantle may be greater than the intellect, but it shouldn't extinguish the intellect."[3] Coverage of Quinn's rebuttal was published in the off-campus student paper, the *Seventh East Press*. This was picked up by *Newsweek* magazine for an article entitled "Apostles vs. Historians," with a photo of Mike Quinn smiling, looking relaxed. This national publicity made Quinn's deconstructive views very visible—he became a public figure overnight. It also heated the brewing conflict between Quinn and Elder Packer, which would continue for two decades.[4]

In 1985, Quinn's *Dialogue* article on post-manifesto polygamy,

---

1. Boyd K. Packer, "The Mantle is Far, Far Greater Than the Intellect," *BYU Studies Quarterly* 21, no. 3 (1981): 259–78.

2. Quinn, "On Being a Mormon Historian," BYU Student History Association, Sep. 1981, archives.lib.byu.edu.

3. A few Mormon historians made this and similar comments at the 1982 Mormon History Association conference.

4. Elbert Peck et al., "Historian Responds to Apostle," *Seventh East Press,* Nov. 1981, 1; Kenneth Woodward, "Apostles vs. Historians," *Newsweek*, Feb. 15, 1982, 51.

"LDS Church Authority and New Plural Marriages, 1890–1904," deconstructed the twentieth-century view of polygamy as an apostate practice outside of the LDS Church. Mike's research showed that polygamy continued inside the LDS Church after the 1890 "manifesto" had denounced polygamy. It was still practiced into the twentieth century by LDS leaders and members who secretly entered or approved at least 250 new polygamous marriages between 1890 and 1904, when a "second manifesto" arose to discourage it.[5] (He pushed this post-manifesto date well into the 1920s as his research on polygamy continued over the years; this was the subject of his final book, uncompleted when he died).

Quinn's 1985 article on polygamy was the first published work that caused problems for his church status. Elder Packer instructed Quinn's local church leader to revoke his LDS temple recommend (which he held onto since Mike needed it for employment at BYU). The following year, in 1986, likely in response to Quinn's research on polygamy, the Church Historical Department began requiring researchers to sign an agreement allowing church review and approval of any planned publications using LDS archival materials. Quinn refused to sign the agreement, which would censor his work; but this meant he couldn't use the LDS archives—a death blow to his research. However, I was willing to sign the agreement, since censorship of my work on the Mormon Trail was unlikely. So Quinn enlisted my help to access materials and check sources in the LDS archives, thus continued using LDS sources without LDS censorship. Mike told me, "I can't afford to pay you, but I can share my research for your projects." I told him, "That's like winning the historical lottery." His mentoring was invaluable. I assisted him from 1986 through the 1990s, since I retained my access to LDS archives in spite of an interrogation in 1989 and excommunication in 1993.

Eventually the church policy of reviewing patrons' work was discontinued by 2004, when Marlin Jensen became executive director and Richard Turley became Assistant Church Historian in 2008. They brought unprecedented openness and access to historical documents. So, after nearly two decades of limited access, during which

5. D. Michael Quinn, "LDS Church Authority and New Plural Marriages, 1890–1904,'" *Dialogue: A Journal of Mormon Thought* 18, no. 1 (Spring 1985): 104.

Quinn produced his most momentous works, he returned to LDS archives, where he was a regular presence until his death in 2021.[6]

The year after Quinn's departure from the archives, in 1987, his most controversial work on LDS history appeared. *Early Mormonism and the Magic World View* radically deconstructed the orthodox view of LDS origins as entirely heaven-sent, instead revealing that the Restoration was equally grounded in human agency. Quinn's massive array of new sources on Mormon origins showed that the faith had arisen not just from the Bible and divine revelation, but also from esoteric traditions that had influenced the Smith family, including folk magic and rituals, divination and dowsing rods, scrying and seer stones, astrology and alchemy, treasure digging, hermeticism, and freemasonry.

Quinn proposed a new paradigm for understanding the emergence of the LDS faith, within early American folk traditions. Church narratives had omitted esoteric or occult influences from which its visionary, mystic, Christian primitivism may have partially sprung, so Quinn recovered them. His intent was not to expose nor embarrass LDS origins as simply occult or weird, but to recover the human processes at work in approaching heavenly powers. He argued that folk magic elements in LDS origins were authentic, normal, and legitimate for early Mormons and Americans, when summoning spiritual experiences and personal revelation.

Early Mormonism and the Magic Worldview dissolved decades of amnesia or avoidance of esoteric practices in LDS roots. In doing so, Quinn deconstructed the dichotomy between orthodoxy vs. heresy by showing that the LDS restoration embodied both. He noted that until the 1850s, only 10–20 percent of Americans were "churched"; thus, the vast majority of people, 80–90 percent, had practiced folk religion.[7]

Quinn both excavated and repeated Joseph Smith's approach to religion, which integrated formal and folk religion, Christianity and esotericism, orthodoxy and heresy, and the canonical with apocryphal. He both revealed and recreated Joseph's religious alchemy—the

---

6. Gary Topping, *D. Michael Quinn: Mormon Historian* (Signature Books, 2022), 123; also, Jennifer Cornelius helped me pinpoint this timeframe.

7. D. Michael Quinn, *Early Mormonism and the Magic World View*, 2nd ed. (Salt Lake City: Signature Books, 1997), xv.

integration or reconciliation of opposites. The book was so startling that it ignited loathing from leaders, attacks from apologists, and critiques from fellow scholars. It shattered the standard LDS paradigm, offering a far larger one. Quinn's scope of sources in *Magic World View* were seemingly superhuman, but he relied on the Philosophical Research Society in Los Angeles, an archive created by Manly Hall in the 1930s. "The PRS enabled me to do the book," he explained, "since most of the esoteric sources were in one place, which made them easy to access."[8]

Quinn and I collaborated in 1989–92 on *Women and Authority: Re-emerging Mormon Feminism,* when I asked him to write an article about LDS women's possession of priesthood. He felt he lacked time to write it, but he owed me research, and I needed his expertise to give our feminist theology more gravity. So we started with his brief *Sunstone* review of Linda Newell's work on women and priesthood, then expanded it into an entirely new and major work, via endless drafts and phone calls between New Orleans and Salt Lake for two to three years. Each time he would add material, he'd say, "How's that?" And I would say, "It doesn't go far enough, we need more evidence and claims." He said I reminded him of the hungry child in Oliver Twist, and I was "the only editor who ever *added* footnotes" to his work. We argued, strategized, and embedded quips like, "A women does not need an appendage to have priesthood." In the end, I got a female priesthood manifesto and he got feminist theory. Whether generous or self-protective, he cited the article as "a collaborative effort."[9]

His article, "Mormon Women Have Had the Priesthood since 1843," deconstructed the twentieth-century church view that LDS men possessed priesthood but that women did not. Quinn documented that women as well as men were anointed and ordained to priesthood in Joseph Smith's Nauvoo sacred rites during 1842–44. He also demonstrated that the women and men themselves understood their priesthood ordinations and practices as real, and also as equivalent in authority. He refuted the notion of male-only

---

8. Private conversation with Mike Quinn in 2004.

9. "If Mormon Women Have Had the Priesthood since 1843, Why Aren't They Using It?," author panel on *Women and Authority,* Sunstone Symposium, Aug. 1993.

priesthood, showing it as a false dichotomy by revealing the inclusion of both genders in LDS priesthood, as originally intended and practiced by Joseph Smith and others in the nineteenth century.

Church reaction to his article and my book in 1993 was extreme. After the volume appeared in January, Quinn and I were summoned in February for questioning by our stake president about our writings. An area Seventy privately shared insights about the apostolic concerns over Quinn's work. "The issue with Quinn is his intent and motivation," he charged; "if someone keeps coming up with negative or embarrassing stuff, you have to wonder about that person's motivations—those *motivations* must be bad … the senior Apostles are very concerned about Quinn … frankly, I'm surprised and impressed at the Church's enormous patience with Quinn."[10]

A decade of Quinn's deconstructive histories had pushed Apostle Packer too far. It was a tragic misperception: an assumption of ill intent on Mike's part, when the real problem was an unbridgeable gap between institutional and scholarly perspectives. When our stake president requested to interview both Quinn and myself, Quinn refused to attend but I was willing to meet and discuss concerns. However, my attempt to alleviate church fears failed. In early May, our Salt Lake Area Seventy, Loren Dunn, summoned both of us to meet with him. Once again, Mike refused to attend while I was willing to meet and hear Dunn's views. And once again, my attempt to solve concerns failed. I asked Elder Dunn why the brethren disliked our work. He said, "It gave us heartburn." He requested that we stop publishing feminist views, which he insisted "serve no purpose." I had to decline his request.

We each were summoned to a high council disciplinary hearing in September 1993. This time we both refused to attend. Quinn had been summoned to formal church disciplinary councils three times that year, which itself was a magic formula. The leaders tried to conjure Mike's presence for church probation, disfellowshipping, and excommunication, but he never appeared—he just kept slipping away. Also summoned that September were Lavina Fielding Anderson, Lynne Whitesides, Avraham Gileadi and Paul Toscano,

10. Dr. Arland Thornton, transcript of his 1993 conversation with an Area Seventy regarding Michael Quinn; copy in my possession.

all of whom were excommunicated, except Whitesides, who was disfellowshipped. Quinn and I were excommunicated for our writings in *Women and Authority* as well as our statements in the media, but mainly for not showing up to our disciplinary court (according to the stake president).

This church confrontation with dissenting scholars and feminists in 1993 was inevitable. Leaders had to deal with discourse that engaged the feared, repressed, unseen aspects of its history, identity, and tradition. Or at least they had to deal with those who had been dealing with those aspects of Mormonism. Elder Packer's May 1993 speech to church leaders named three "dangers" to the church: scholars, feminists, and homosexuals.[11] He therefore did the church a favor by identifying the LDS shadow (the feared, avoided, rejected self) and its shadow workers—as scholars, feminists, and gays.

Other scholars and feminists were subjected to church discipline in 1993 and throughout the rest of the decade. Some lost jobs, status, or membership. Quinn had left BYU in 1988 so he couldn't be fired, but professors David Knowlton, Cecelia Konchar Farr, and Gail Turley Houston all lost their jobs at the university, while Eugene England, Scott Abbott, Martha Bradley, and Martha Beck felt constrained to resign from BYU. Excommunications continued in 1994 for scholars Brent Metcalfe and David Wright, as well as in 1995 for feminist Janice Allred, followed by professor Margaret Toscano in 2000. The 1990s endured a series of traumatic church collisions with itself—its history, theology and dissenting members. It was only after this that the church began embracing public scholarly discussion of itself in 2001.

The church's public encounter with dissenting and deconstructive work on Mormonism in the 1980s and 1990s needed scapegoats to absorb the shock of disorientation and discomfort. It took time to acclimate to revisionist history and theology in less traumatic and more productive ways. Michael Quinn's deconstructive work was always at the forefront of that confrontation, making him a scapegoat for the church. The burden of blame, fear, and shunning for shattering the status quo was devastating for him personally and

---

11. Boyd K. Packer, "All-Church Coordinating Council Meeting" May 18, 1993, archive.org.

professionally. He suffered every possible loss to his career, income, reputation, family life, and self-image. Few people knew the toll this took on Quinn's life, since he endured it all with uncommon grace.

Undaunted, Quinn continued producing momentous work through the 1990s. His 1996 book, *Same-Sex Dynamics among Nineteenth-Century Americans: A Mormon Example*, again deconstructed institutional twentieth-century LDS views, this time on homosexuality. His groundbreaking history revealed that queerness, homosocial dynamics, and same-sex relationships were tolerated or accepted in the nineteenth-century LDS Church, rather than seen as indecent, perverse, or scandalous, even as late as the 1930s and '40s. He documented same-sex society, discourse, and behavior in Mormon culture, even among some prominent church leaders.

The evidence for Quinn's assertions were myriad. He noted that Brigham Young preferred men-only dances, and that Mormon Tabernacle Choir director Evan Stevens and Church Patriarch Joseph F. Smith entertained some degree of same-sex relationships. He documented that Mormon attitudes toward same-sex dynamics were as tolerant as those across the U.S. and Europe—until the Oscar Wilde trial of 1895 in England triggered hostility for queerness on both continents. Quinn deconstructed the view of homosexuality as Other, by revealing that Mormonism itself had been rather queer.

In 1998, Quinn released his second edition of *The Magic World View*, which added 400 pages, including a response to his critics, accusing them of polemics rather than engagement of his evidence. He sharply condemned a "polemicist" as "a dishonorable vocation" charging that "polemics intentionally destroys the give and take of sincerely respectful disagreement."[12] Throughout, he validated apologetics as honest self-defense, while decrying polemics as distortive personal attacks.

Last, Quinn's magna opera in 1994, 1997, and 2017, *The Mormon Hierarchy* trilogy, stunningly revised the history of LDS authority, leadership, and finances, by excavating their structures, tensions, complexities and the subverted, unknown aspects of each. He also lauded the inspiration and internal integrity inhabiting those structures due

---

12. Quinn, *Early Mormonism*, x.

to Joseph Smith's intentions, capacity, and work to establish a balanced and egalitarian church within hierarchical scaffolding.

Volume one, *Origins of Power* (1994), revised our understanding of Joseph Smith's and Brigham Young's different approaches to church leadership, revealing a drastic shift after Smith died. Quinn traced Smith's leading "decision-making bodies" and officers as designed to counterbalance each other; yet Young consolidated top authority in the Twelve Apostles and himself as president, subverting Joseph's balance of powers and genders. Quinn showed that although Young sought to complete Smith's religious goals and structures, he changed them in ways that diminished or reversed their intended functioning. This caused Emma Smith to lament in August 1844 that her husband's lay church was gone, declaring "there is no church."[13]

Volume two, *Extensions of Power* (1997), reconsidered the evolution of authority during and after Young's reign, until the late twentieth century, and revealed the underlying agendas and tensions in church leadership. Quinn deconstructed idealized notions of infallible leaders and a unified Quorum of Apostles, documenting their contrasting personalities and conflicts which opposed each other in complex power dynamics, while presenting a unified front. He traced revisions in church positions, policy and identity that subverted its visionary and mystic origins.

Volume three, *Wealth and Corporate Power* (2017), was forty years in the making, a lone sojourn through a desert of hidden data. Quinn persisted in recovering inaccessible and exhaustingly complex historical details on LDS business and finances. He showed that church leaders from the beginning had created enterprises that benefitted the church, as well as themselves. For example, Brigham Young had a million dollars when he died in 1877, an amount then considered a rare, colossal fortune. Quinn listed endless enterprises created, managed, or owned by the church or its leaders, which ran the gamut from railroads to hotels, from lumber, woolen, and sugar mills to dairies and clothiers. There were countless companies on paper only, with the same church leaders' names on the boards. However, he also firmly attested that

---

13. William Clayton, diary, Aug. 27, 1844, qtd. in George D. Smith, *An Intimate Chronicle: The Journals of William Clayton* 2nd ed. (Salt Lake City: Signature Books, 1995), 143–44, 145–46.

church financial recovery and growth in the twentieth century was a truly miraculous story, unexplainable by business management alone.

The significance and impact of Michael Quinn's deconstructions of false dichotomies and illegitimate privilege, which he believed had betrayed Mormonism's radically inclusive origins, cannot be overstated. His work excavated the foundations of LDS faith in ways that recovered its most unique, distinctive—yet forgotten—elements and syntheses. He recovered the rejected or lost dimensions of Mormon identity, complexity, and inspiration, along with the flaws, mistakes, harms. He revealed the profound paradoxes that inhabit Mormon origins and evolution, and refuted the polemics that responded to those paradoxes.

If I had to pick the most crucial deconstructions in Quinn's immense body of work, it would be these four: his recovery of Mormonism's marriage of esoteric tradition with Christian religion in *Early Mormonism and the Magic World View*; the historic equality of LDS women's ordination in "Mormon Women Have Had the Priesthood since 1843"; the historic inclusion of LDS queerness documented in *Same Sex Dynamics*; and finally, his excavation and deconstruction of apostolic hegemony in 1844–47 that subverted Mormonism's original intended balance of authority, power, and gender as documented in *Origins of Power*.

Michael Quinn was as deconstructive in his own life and identity as he was in his writings. He described himself as "born with a split identity," meaning he embodied opposites—Anglo and Latino, LDS and Catholic, an academic in a working-class family, a professor made in the military, a voice of authority from the margins, a queer studies scholar with essentialist views, a heretic critic and orthodox believer, a linear thinker and mystic visionary, a gay male feminist. He was all three of Elder Packer's most feared "dangers" to Mormonism. Yet it was those intersecting identities within him that enabled him to see and value all perspectives.[14]

Quinn's innate gift for paradox made him a deconstructive person, much like Joseph Smith, with whom he identified. They shared the view that by reconciling or "proving contraries, truth is made

---

14. Quinn, "On Being a Mormon Historian (and Its Aftermath)," in *Faithful History*, ed. George D. Smith (Salt Lake City: Signature Books, 1992).

manifest"—a deeper or fuller truth.[15] They both sought "to receive truth, let it come from whence it may … [and] gather all the good and true principles in the world and treasure them up, or we shall not come out true 'Mormons.'"[16] Michael Quinn was, indeed, a true Mormon.

Significantly, Quinn relied upon both intellectual and spiritual methods in his research. His 1981 BYU speech attested that he had "always researched and written about church history with a continual prayer for the Lord to guide him in knowing what to do and how to express things."[17] I once asked him, "Do you ever feel like someone is standing on the other side of the veil, handing documents to you?" "Yes!" he affirmed. "How do you think I find all those sources?" He explained that each time he started a project, he prayed for divine direction to guide him to what he needed—and it came, over and over again. He believed that he was spiritually called, destined and aided to research and write the works he produced. He always credited divine assistance for his articles and books.

Michael Quinn's fifty-year role as LDS historical gadfly and human deconstructive lever did not make him simply a tragic figure, as he is often portrayed due to his lack of academic position. His body of work was an extraordinary success beyond that of many scholars with institutional positions. Quinn did everything he was destined to do in Mormon studies, which the demands of an academic job might have limited. The church may never agree with all that Mike saw and wrote, but it will always be there, in his texts.

In 2011, Quinn was invited by the LDS Church History Library to consult with their team on research about polygamy, particularly post-manifesto polygamy. This event brought him full circle: from the first article that got him in trouble with the church in 1985, to being sought by the church for assistance on that same topic twenty-five years later. Rather than balk at the extraordinary irony, Quinn was thrilled to be needed, valued, and useful to the church. It was a healing event for both him and the church.

Likewise, my return to LDS Church membership in 2012 was

15. *History of the Church,* 6:428.

16. History, 1838–1856, volume E-1 [1 July 1843–30 April 1844] https://www. josephsmithpapers.org/paper-summary/history-1838-1856-volume-e-1-1-july-1843-30-april-1844/51.

17. Quinn, "On Being a Mormon Historian."

aided by Quinn who validated and coached my process of rebaptism. We were partners in excommunication, then partners again in re-communication, as I exerted to heal what had happened twenty years earlier in 1993. He recognized a higher purpose and synchronicity in my return, which caused him to consider returning, himself. However, he chose not to reconcile, though I was willing. He could not abide the church policy on LGBTQs as a member. I understood why it felt wrong for him to return. And he understood why it felt right for me.

He told me later, after I wrote to Elder Packer about returning, "You are in a unique position to build bridges of listening, understanding, empathy, and reconciliation with LDS leaders. I commend you for this and pray for your continued success. As indication of my own limits and weakness, I could NOT be the bridge-builder with Elder Packer that you have been. His letter to you was sweet and important. Hugs, Mike."[18] Quinn embraced my rebaptism in spite of his own unsolvable alienation. He honored my journey and its paradox, with Christlike wisdom and grace as always.

Yet, Quinn too found reconciliation with the church, in another way. When a whistleblower publicly shared documents in 2019 that revealed LDS Church tithing investments totaled at least 100 billion dollars, I called Quinn to tell him the news and send him the articles, which disclosed financial figures he had tried for years to acquire. Given his expertise on church finance, the media sought him for comment.[19] As always, he gave deeply informed and objective insights on the controversy. He defended the investment funds as necessary to keep the church and its work fully afloat, and stable in the future. He also affirmed that, in "the larger picture ... the church is not a profit-making business," and that church finances are actually "an enormously faith-promoting story."[20] When his com-

---

18. Michael Quinn, email to the author, May 9, 2013.

19. "Mormon Church Has Misled Members on $100 Billion Tax-Exempt Investment Fund, Whistleblower Alleges," *Washington Post*, Dec. 17, 2019; also, "Whistleblower Claims That LDS Church Stockpiled 100 Billion Dollars," *Salt Lake Tribune*, Dec. 17, 2019.

20. "Historian Digs into the Hidden World of Mormon Finances, Shows How Church Went from Losing Money to Making Money—Lots of It," *Salt Lake Tribune*, Oct. 14, 2017.

ments were quoted by the LDS Church Newsroom in defense of the church, along with a description and link to his book *The Mormon Hierarchy: Wealth and Corporate Power* on amazon.com, I called to give him the extraordinary news.[21]

Rather than lament any personal injustice, Quinn was ecstatic to learn that his work had been used by the church to defend itself against unfair criticism. For him, his apologetic was more about deconstructing polemics than about defending the institution. He was thrilled that his historical work was finally recognized by the church as vital analysis of LDS history, functioning and controversy. Quinn offered a deeper, objective perspective on the realities of church finance—as well as his testimony of it as a truly miraculous story.

I told him, "You realize what this means—you've just been reinstated by the church, without rebaptism." He loved that, and agreed, that the church's public reconciliation with his relentlessly honest, probing, revisionist historical work had reversed the reason for his excommunication—and that was even better than baptism.

21. LDS Church Newsroom, "How the Church of Jesus Christ Uses Tithing and Funds," Dec. 20, 2019; *Church News*, "An Inside Look at How Church Finances Fund Worldwide Efforts…" Dec. 2019.

An Unlikely Conservative: D. Michael Quinn on Latter-day Saint Leadership and Hierarchy

PATRICK Q. MASON AND HOVAN LAWTON

By almost any measure, the leadership of the Church of Jesus Christ of Latter-day Saints—and especially its all-male priesthood hierarchy—was the central concern for D. Michael Quinn during his influential career as one of Mormonism's leading historians. Certainly his contributions in other areas were substantial, as the other essays in this volume attest, but no other subject occupied his sustained attention as did the LDS Church's leadership. Quinn's interest in this topic began in his youth then culminated in a voluminous body of scholarship, including an MA thesis, PhD dissertation, five books, and numerous articles that focused primarily on documenting the personalities, processes, and perils attendant to "the Mormon hierarchy."

There is an irony in this. Because of his excommunication from the church, Michael Quinn has often been understood by both admirers and critics as a dissenter or even rebel. To be sure, he was willing to publish material from the archives that exposed the all-too-human side of Latter-day Saint hierarchs in his dogged pursuit of historical truth. However, he never lost faith that heaven was somehow mysteriously working in and through a church led by mortal, fallible men. Quinn believed that his scholarship promoted rather than denigrated Mormonism's foundational truths, including the fundamental teaching that God calls prophets and apostles in modern times. He was critical of authoritarianism and wary of the reflexive "follow the prophet" mentality that overtook the church during his lifetime. Nevertheless, he never abandoned his belief that there was something fundamentally integral, even inspired, about the nature and structure of the Latter-day Saint hierarchy in its purest form. Most strikingly, Quinn believed for years that he was

71

destined to join the senior quorums of church leadership. This out-look seemingly shaped his research interests and also inclined him toward a sympathetic view of leaders' intentions, if not always their words and actions.

Quinn's fascination with the leadership of the LDS Church was evident from the outset of his training and career as a histo-rian. That native interest was fueled by his access to a bonanza of newly available institutional records, diaries, and other documents in the church's archives that afforded him unprecedented insights into Mormon history. He wrote his 1973 master's thesis at the Uni-versity of Utah on the topic of "Organizational Development and Social Origins of the Mormon Hierarchy, 1832–1932." His doctoral dissertation, completed three years later, was similarly titled, "The Mormon Hierarchy, 1832–1932: An American Elite." This work would become the basis for his three-volume *Mormon Hierarchy* se-ries; the arguments remained substantially similar, even while his later published books compounded additional evidence and exam-ples for support. Along the way, he also published two biographies of J. Reuben Clark. While each of these five books deserve individ-ualized treatment, here we consider a few key themes that cut across all of Quinn's work on the Latter-day Saint hierarchy.

First, Quinn argued that the distinctive features of Latter-day Saint leadership had revealed origins. As he stated in his disser-tation, "the essential starting point for Mormon political theory is within the standard works of LDS scripture."[1] On one level this seems to be an unremarkable sentence. Just as scholars often look to the Hebrew Bible, New Testament, and Qur'an to illuminate the respective origins and nature of Jewish, Christian, and Muslim organizational and leadership structures, Mormon studies scholars frequently turn to Joseph Smith's revelatory productions to iden-tify the origins of various aspects of Latter-day Saint thought and practice. Yet Quinn was often content to stop at what Restoration scripture said, and not explore what other cultural or religious influ-ences may have impacted the original notions and development of Latter-day Saint leadership.

---

1. D. Michael Quinn, "The Mormon Hierarchy, 1832–1932: An American Elite," (PhD diss., Yale University, 1976), 158.

Largely ignoring broader contexts was a conscious decision on Quinn's part. In the introduction to *Extensions of Power*, he wrote that early in his career he had planned on situating his findings on the Mormon hierarchy both theoretically within "elite theory in political science" and comparatively "with group biographies of elites in various enterprises and cultures." Other scholars encouraged him to apply organizational behavior theory, the anthropology or sociology of religion, or religious studies theory. Quinn determined, however, "that it is necessary to establish the data before seeking larger contexts." His would be a "primarily descriptive" project; "I leave it to others," he said, "to provide the comparative analysis and new insights" based on the data he compiled and published.[2] In this respect, many other historians—Richard Bushman perhaps being the most prominent—have offered readers far more by way of the broader context for the development of early Mormon structures and hierarchies, tracing various secular and religious counterparts, parallels, and influences.[3] Social scientists have weighed in with useful theoretical models, such as Michael McBride's analysis of authority in Mormonism using rational choice theory.[4] In short, the world of Quinn's Mormon hierarchy was exhaustively detailed but curiously self-defining, though it provided a foundation for later work.

Second, Quinn was interested in complicating what official church histories had often presented as a rather flat narrative of continuity and consistency. His writings on Latter-day Saint leadership were always attendant to change over time, especially the trend toward increased hierarchy, theocracy, and bureaucratization. In the very first issue of the *Journal of Mormon History*, for instance, Quinn echoed Thomas O'Dea's characterization of Mormonism as evolving from "master-disciple" relationships to a more organized hierarchy, while

---

2. D. Michael Quinn, *The Mormon Hierarchy: Extensions of Power* (Salt Lake City: Signature Books, 1997), ix.

3. See Richard Lyman Bushman, *Joseph Smith: Rough Stone Rolling* (New York: Alfred A. Knopf, 2005); Bushman, "Joseph Smith and Power," in *A Firm Foundation: Church Organization and Administration*, ed. David J. Whittaker and Arnold K. Garr (Provo, UT: Religious Studies Center, Brigham Young University/ Salt Lake City: Deseret Book, 2011), 1–13.

4. See Michael McBride, "Authority in Mormonism: A Rational Choice Analysis," in *Directions for Mormon Studies in the Twenty-First Century*, ed. Patrick Q. Mason (Salt Lake City: University of Utah Press, 2016), 179–203.

ten years later he wrote in *Dialogue* that the religion shifted from "authoritarian democracy to an authoritarian oligarchy."[5] Quinn was especially troubled by what he (and others) identified as a marked shift toward centralized authority beginning in the 1960s, a move centered doctrinally (or at least discursively) on a new emphasis on the quasi-infallibility of Mormon prophets. Again, for the most part, Quinn was content to document these trends rather than theorize them. It was not a historian but a sociologist, Armand Mauss, who most famously made theoretical sense of the move toward "retrenchment" in the last third of the twentieth century.[6]

Third, Quinn challenged institutional church histories that have emphasized harmony among the senior leadership. Dissidents are occasionally acknowledged, but their role in official histories has primarily been to emphasize the dangers of dissent and importance of loyalty to God's chosen prophets. As part of the vanguard of the new Mormon history, Quinn was a pioneer in documenting the persistent and sometimes debilitating conflicts that existed within and between the church's presiding quorums. He suggested that much if not most of this conflict occurred because of overlapping and sometimes unclear ecclesiastical jurisdictions that later got sorted—sometimes only to create new conflicts. Due to his access to previously restricted private papers, Quinn was one of the first to pull back the curtain on the internal conflict and contestation that existed among the senior leadership for the church's first century and a half; perhaps only Gary Bergera and Greg Prince have made similarly significant contributions in this area.[7]

Fourth, and to a degree that has not been paralleled by any other scholar, Quinn traced the dynastic elements present in senior church quorums throughout the nineteenth and twentieth centuries. Interestingly, Quinn generally defended the church's leadership from

---

5. D. Michael Quinn, "The Evolution of the Presiding Quorums of the Church," *Journal of Mormon History* 1 (1974): 21–34; Quinn, "From Sacred Grove to Sacral Power Structures," *Dialogue: A Journal of Mormon Thought* 17, no. 2 (Summer 1984): 16.

6. See Armand L. Mauss, *The Angel and the Beehive: The Mormon Struggle with Assimilation* (Urbana: University of Illinois Press, 1994).

7. Gary Bergera, *Conflict in the Quorum: Orson Pratt, Brigham Young, Joseph Smith*, 2nd ed. (Salt Lake City: Signature Books, 2017); Gregory A. Prince and Wm. Robert Wright, *David O. McKay and the Rise of Modern Mormonism* (Salt Lake City: University of Utah Press, 2005).

charges of simple nepotism. In *Extensions of Power*, he argued that the "dynasticism" present among the senior leadership was not only to be expected, given how small the church was and the doctrinal emphasis on family ties and relationships, but also that it contributed "additional unity, stability, and loyalty" to the early Mormon movement. He further pushed back against the nepotism narrative by pointing to excommunications and disciplinary measures taken toward individual leaders from prominent families, and affirmed that "personal worthiness" was the most important factor in the selection of senior church leaders.[8]

Fifth, though researching and writing in an era in which the American historical profession had made a decisive turn toward social history, cultural history, women's history, and African American history, Quinn produced an impressive and foundational catalog of scholarship that by and large kept the beliefs and behaviors of elite white men at the center of Mormon history. The narrowness of his focus is both expected and revealing. That there are almost no people of color may be understandable in a series of studies on the first century and a half of Mormon leadership. That women are present but not central in many of his studies tells us something of what Quinn counted as Mormon leadership. The option to more extensively include the voices and experiences of female leaders was available to him: Quinn had access to all the documents that Jill Derr, Carol Cornwall Madsen, and other pioneering Latter-day Saint women's historians did. He simply chose to focus on the church's male priesthood elite. In more recent decades, scholars like Derr, Madsen, Catherine Brekus, Dave Hall, and Laurel Thatcher Ulrich have broadened our understanding of female leadership within the church.[9]

---

8. Quinn, *Extensions of Power*, 196–97.

9. See Jill Mulvay Derr, Janath Russell Cannon, and Maureen Ursenbach Beecher, *Women of Covenant: The Story of Relief Society* (Salt Lake City and Provo, UT: Deseret Book Company and Brigham Young University Press, 1992); Carol Cornwall Madsen, *An Advocate for Women: The Public Life of Emmeline B. Wells, 1870–1920* (Provo, UT: Brigham Young University Press, 2006); Catherine Brekus, "Mormon Women and the Problem of Historical Agency," *Journal of Mormon History* 37, no. 2 (Spring 2011): 58–87; Dave Hill, *A Faded Legacy: Amy Brown Lyman and Mormon Women's Activism, 1872–1959* (Salt Lake City: University of Utah Press, 2015); Laurel Thatcher Ulrich, *A House Full of Females: Plural Marriage and Women's Rights in Early Mormonism* (New York: Knopf, 2017).

Finally, while he could be unsparing in his criticism of church hierarchs—whether it be the violence of nineteenth-century leaders or the objectification of individuals that he saw as motivating the principal architects of Mormonism's "baseball baptism" era[10]— Quinn's portrayal of church leadership was largely sympathetic. With a few exceptions, he saw their motivations as being grounded in sincere religiosity and a genuine desire to build the kingdom of God in anticipation of Jesus Christ's Second Coming. This was perhaps most evident in the third and final volume of the *Mormon Hierarchy* series, the 2017 volume subtitled *Wealth and Corporate Power*. Many expected Quinn's last book to be an exposé of institutional corruption and personal enrichment. Instead, critics of the church were disappointed when Quinn characterized his four-decade investigation into church finances as ultimately being "an enormously faith-promoting story."[11]

When assessing Michael Quinn's historiographical legacy, this last point should not be underemphasized. If during the course of Quinn's life historians often doubled as theologians within the Church of Jesus Christ of Latter-day Saints—if only for lack of better options—then Quinn was the church's preeminent historian-theologian of the belief that LDS prophets and apostles are simultaneously fallible and followable. In his opening to both of his J. Reuben Clark biographies, Quinn made the following statement (quoted here from the 2002 volume, *Elder Statesman*, published nearly a decade after his excommunication): "I should disclose my own belief that the general authorities of the Church of Jesus Christ of Latter-day Saints are called [to] their positions by divine guidance, and I am confident that they seek to carry out their administrative responsibilities by that inspiration. I also believe in the important truth expressed by President Clark to LDS religion teachers at Brigham Young University, 'Yet we must not forget that prophets are mortal men, with men's infirmities.'" Quinn wrote his

---

10. See D. Michael Quinn, *The Mormon Hierarchy: Origins of Power* (Salt Lake City: Signature Books, 1994), 92–103; Quinn, *Extensions of Power*, 226–61; Quinn, "I-Thou vs. I-It Conversions: The Mormon 'Baseball Baptism' Era," *Sunstone*, Dec. 1993, 30–44.

11. Peggy Fletcher Stack, "Historian Digs into the Hidden World of Mormon Finances, Shows How Church Went from Losing Money to Making Money—Lots of It," *Salt Lake Tribune*, Oct. 14, 2017.

Clark biography, and arguably his entire corpus, trying "to maintain the balanced viewpoint which [Clark] recommended."[12]

In this respect, Michael Quinn's scholarship on LDS elites is perhaps best understood as being fundamentally conservative. "Conservative" here is not meant in the political or theological sense; indeed, ardent fans of Ezra Taft Benson won't find much to celebrate in Quinn's treatment of their arch-conservative hero.[13] Rather, Quinn's abundant body of work on Latter-day Saint leadership was conservative in the broader sense of preserving the authority and integrity of traditional structures and relationships. He wrote about white male religious elites, traced the origins of LDS leadership structures to God, assumed the best intentions of most leaders, sympathized with the outcomes of their decision-making even when things turned out poorly, and critiqued a turn toward authoritarianism (whether in Danites, Brigham Young, or Boyd K. Packer) that he saw as betraying the true, divinely revealed nature of prophetic leadership in Christ's restored church. If anything, the meta-narrative in Quinn's work was one of spiritual declension, maintaining there was a core of spiritual truth in Joseph Smith's revelations that remains intact despite later giving way to more authoritarian, bureaucratic forms.[14] Though critical, Quinn's perspective fundamentally reifies rather than deconstructs Mormonism as a divinely revealed religious system. In other words, his account of declension functions more as mournful lament for what has been lost (or accreted) than an angry denunciation of a propagated fraud.

Historians' work often has some relationship to their own autobiography. Without going too far down the road of psychohistory, we might consider the possibility that Michael Quinn was so fascinated—at times, seemingly obsessed—by Mormon leaders precisely because for much of his life he fully expected to become one himself. At the impressionable age of nine, his grandmother told him that

---

12. D. Michael Quinn, *Elder Statesman: A Biography of J. Reuben Clark* (Salt Lake City: Signature Books, 2002), xviii.

13. See especially Quinn, *Extensions of Power*, 66–115.

14. This view is evident, for instance, in Quinn's essay "Mormon Women Have Had the Priesthood since 1843," in *Women and Authority: Re-emerging Mormon Feminism*, ed. Maxine Hanks (Salt Lake City, UT: Signature Books, 1992), 365–409.

he would become an LDS apostle someday.[15] This feeling was reinforced years later by spiritual feelings shared with a friend that the two of them would both become apostles and even serve together in the First Presidency.[16]

For Quinn, these were not idle speculations or wishes. In January 1973, just as he was beginning his career as a historian in earnest, Quinn sought out Spencer W. Kimball—then president of the Quorum of the Twelve Apostles—for counsel and a blessing. Quinn remembered his twenty-nine-year-old self specifically wanting Kimball to provide relief from his unrelenting "thoughts of becoming an apostle" and "seeking church office," which Quinn interpreted as "an expression of my lifelong pride and arrogance." (It's worth noting that Quinn entirely internalizes this expectation, and does not contextualize it within a broader aspiration to leadership so common among many Mormon men of his generation.) When at the end of their hourlong meeting Kimball laid his hands on the young historian's head, the blessing he pronounced was not the one that Quinn sought. Rather than releasing him of his anxiety-producing expectations, Quinn later remembered, "instead [Kimball] promised me that I would one day be an apostle." Quinn was "devastated"—as was his wife Jan, who "sobbed for hours" upon hearing Mike's report of the meeting. Quinn sincerely believed that Spencer W. Kimball was an apostle of the Lord. While the apostle's blessing defied any "rational understanding," even four decades later Quinn still testified, "I do not expect anyone else to understand that experience, but I can't doubt it. ... I certainly don't understand it," but "I can't doubt the inspiration that he gave."[17]

It does not take great effort or imagination to connect the dots between Quinn's psyche and spiritual expectations, prophetically confirmed at the beginning of the year in which he would write his master's thesis, and his lifelong interest in the Mormon hierarchy.

---

15. See D. Michael Quinn, *Chosen Path: A Memoir* (Salt Lake City: Signature Books, forthcoming), entry for July 1953. See also David Haglund, "The Case of the Mormon Historian," *Slate*, Nov. 1, 2012.

16. Quinn, *Chosen Path*, entry for June 14, 1972.

17. D. Michael Quinn, "D. Michael Quinn: Special Witness," interview with Bill Reel, *Mormon Discussion* podcast, episode 161, July 30, 2015. See also Quinn, *Chosen Path*, entry for Jan. 23, 1973.

Whether at the front or back of his mind, Quinn's research and writing about LDS Church leadership seems to have been in part an effort to document the history of the group of elites he anticipated one day being a part of.

D. Michael Quinn's scholarship illuminates and embodies the paradox that has haunted liberal and progressive Mormons (including many intellectuals) ever since the 1960s: how does one espouse democratic, inclusive values while simultaneously believing in, participating in, and writing about a religious system that concentrates power in an all-male ecclesiastical hierarchy? Though bravely piloting a number of pioneering low-orbit flights that offer crucial perspectives, Quinn could never quite escape the powerful gravitational pull of the male LDS priesthood hierarchy. It is, admittedly, an extremely vexing task, one that many of Mormonism's very best scholars continue to grapple with. It's not just any hierarchy that is built into the Latter-day Saint ecclesiastical system—it is a distinctly gendered hierarchy, one that was also deeply racialized for most of Mormon history and arguably remains so today.

The entire Mormon historical community owes an enormous debt to D. Michael Quinn for his pioneering, forthright, and often courageous scholarship exploring, in his words, the previously "uncharted terrain of the Mormon hierarchy's experience."[18] Now, a generation later, it is our task to build upon the deep engagement with archival sources that Quinn so excelled at. We have the opportunity to do exactly what he called for, to "provide the comparative analysis and new insights" that are produced when rigorous archival research is combined with broader contextualization, intersectional analysis, and diverse theoretical lenses. No matter what comes next, one thing is sure: Quinn's influence on the study of Mormon leadership and hierarchy looms so large that his name will always appear in future footnotes. That legacy, no doubt, is enough to make him smile.

---

18. Quinn, *Extensions of Power*, ix.

Persisting Magic: Situating Early Mormonism and the Magic World View in Mormon Studies

IAN BARBER

There is a famous whakataukī (proverb) of the Indigenous Māori reo (language) of my homeland that is said when a significant person passes away. That whakataukī introduces this chapter in tribute to my friend, D. Michael Quinn.

Kua hinga he tōtara i Te Waonui-a-Tāne: A tōtara (mighty tree) has fallen in the great forest of (the deity) Tāne.

This chapter situates both editions of D. Michael Quinn's monumental *Early Mormonism and the Magic World View* as contributions to, and from, later twentieth-century Mormon historiography.[1] I evaluate *Early Mormonism* in the context of late twentieth century thinking on Joseph Smith's religious work and movement. As well, I assess the twenty-first century legacy and enduring value of Quinn's study for Latter-day Saints scholarship and culture.

Mormonism, "Folk Magic," and Scholarship: Origins

It is an understatement to say that "magic" as an analytical construct has been much debated across religious studies, anthropology, and history, especially its relationship to religion. Both editions of *Early Mormonism* acknowledged these multi-disciplinary debates. Not without controversy, Quinn settled on standard twentieth-century dictionary definitions, with "magic" describing the use of a means (ceremony, charm, or object) to cause a specific result by supernatural power. These means might include divination, rituals, and

---

1. D. Michael Quinn, *Early Mormonism and the Magic World View* (Salt Lake City: Signature Books, 1987); Quinn, *Early Mormonism and the Magic World View*, 2nd rev. ed. (Salt Lake City: Signature Books, 1998).

(or) objects that are "in themselves powerful," where inorganic or in-animate materials may have "life."[2] It was Quinn's further argument that Old World magical beliefs and practices as recorded in occult manuscripts and manuals of the ancient to early modern periods had "filtered down to the common people" of the North American colonies as incorporated "into their own folklore and folk religion." For Quinn, this explained the young seer's instrumental treasure seeking, as well as some later Mormon practices and ideas.[3]

The 1987 edition of *Early Mormonism* was not the first detailed treatment of the subject. Quinn acknowledged it was the product of "two years research into possible connections between early Mormonism and folk magic, topics to which other researchers have devoted many more years of work."[4] Fawn Brodie's *No Man Knows My History*—enlarged, redistributed, and rediscovered by a new generation of researchers from 1971—had profiled these early connections for post-war scholars of Mormon origins.[5] Brodie had accepted, largely, the neighbor accusations as collected by ex-Mormon Doctor Philastus Hurlbut and collated in Eber D. Howe's 1834 anti-Mormon polemic *Mormonism Unvailed*, though she noted their biased origins. According to these testimonies, Joseph Smith Sr. had directed sacrificial rituals and relied on the scrying abilities and instruments (peep stones or seer stones) of his son Joseph Smith Jr. in the 1820s. For *No Man*, the local scrying folk environment, along with revivalism, was formative for young Joseph. *No Man* portrayed a dismissive, elitist attitude toward the local treasure lore also, claiming that "most bucolic scryers are

---

2. These definitions of magic have been criticized by Latter-day Saints scholars, including reviewers of Quinn, *Early Mormonism*, rev. ed., as being irrelevant to Joseph Smith's early history, incoherent, and inconsistent with current scholarship (e.g., John Gee, "An Obstacle to Better Understanding," *FARMS Review* of Books 12, no. 2 (2000): 185–90; William J. Hamblin, "That Old Black Magic," *FARMS Review of Books* 12, no. 2 (2000): 227–34). However, something like Quinn's applied practice approach at least is recognizable in a recent anthropological definition of magic as a craft or "set of techniques" to transform "self and the world." Matteo Benussi, "Magic," in *The Cambridge Encyclopedia of Anthropology* (2019), anthroencyclopedia.com.

3. Quinn, *Early Mormonism*, 1st ed., xi–xii, xviii.

4. Quinn, *Early Mormonism*, 1st ed., x.

5. Fawn Brodie, *No Man Knows My History: The Life of Joseph Smith*, 2nd rev. ed. (New York: Alfred A. Knopf, 1972).

ignorant, superstitious folk who believe profoundly in their mineral rods and rabbits' feet."[6]

Orthodox Latter-day Saints scholars such as Hugh Nibley and Richard Lloyd Anderson dismissed the published treasure-scrying accusations.[7] But documents uncovered in 1971 led to a reassessment of the influence of magic instruments and expectations on the young Joseph Smith. Reverend Wesley Walters, a determined evangelical researcher on Mormon origins, identified original 1826 bills from a Bainbridge court hearing stored by Norwich County, New York, that related to Joseph Smith's employment by Josiah Stowell to help prospect for a purported Spanish mine.[8] Nibley had rejected later nineteenth-century reports of scrying accusations against Joseph Smith Jr. from the hearing. But they were taken seriously by Brodie, who noted that Joseph's mother, Lucy Mack Smith, recalled that Stowell had come for her son after learning that he was in "possession of certain means, by which he could discern things that could not be seen by the natural eye."[9]

BYU historian Marvin Hill published the first scholarly analysis of the Norwich County bills from copies supplied by Walters in the same year that the second edition of *No Man* appeared. Hill was cautious because of reported irregularities in the recovery of the bills. Even so, Hill's own "preliminary investigation" at the sheriff's office in Norwich confirmed at least that the copies circulated by Walters were similar to other court documents of the time, even though the original documents were unavailable. As if anticipating events to come, Hill added that further research would be necessary to prove

6. Brodie, *No Man*, 31. E. D. Howe, *Mormonism Unvailed: or, A Faithful Account of That Singular Imposition and Delusion, from Its Rise to the Present Time* (Painesville, OH: E. D. Howe, 1834).

7. Hugh Nibley, *The Myth Makers* (Salt Lake City: Bookcraft, 1961); Richard Lloyd Anderson, "Joseph Smith's New York Reputation Reappraised," *BYU Studies* 10, no. 3 (Spring 1970): 283–314.

8. Wesley P. Walters, "Joseph Smith's Bainbridge, N.Y. Court Trials," *Westminster Theological Journal* 36, no. 2 (Winter 1974): 123–55; Marvin S. Hill, "Joseph Smith and the 1826 Trial: New Evidence and New Difficulties," *BYU Studies* 12, no. 2 (Winter 1972): 225, [image] 233.

9. Nibley, *Myth Makers*, 139–57; cf. Brodie, *No Man*, 28–31, 440–41. For a critical text note on Lucy Mack Smith's statement see Lavina Fielding Anderson, ed., *Lucy's Book: A Critical Edition of Lucy Mack Smith's Family Memoir* (Salt Lake City: Signature Books, 2001), 360.

the documents' authenticity. Hill also characterized the idea that Joseph Smith was a "religious fraud" because he sought after gold as a view "of our generation." For Hill, if "an element of mysticism" had led Smith and other Mormons to search for buried treasure, "it does not disprove the genuineness of their religious convictions."[10]

Two church histories published by the newly professionalized LDS Historical Department in the 1970s acknowledged evidence of Smith's treasure seeking and the 1826 court hearing, but only to identify one of his "curious sidelines," or to argue for participation in activities "as innocent and prevalent in the 1820s" as astrology is today.[11] In 1977, Joseph Smith biographer Donna Hill, Marvin Hill's sister, also summarized the records of the 1826 hearings and other early evidence of Smith's treasure seeking and belief in seer stones.[12] Reflecting her brother's views, Hill added that "respected citizens and church goers" dug for treasure in New England and western New York, and "saw no conflict between that and their religious convictions."[13]

The theme was explored further in a landmark 1984 study of Mormon beginnings by LDS historian Richard Bushman. In Bushman's history, the 1820s Smith family believed in the "invisible powers" of scripture and were then "no more able to distinguish true religion from superstition than their neighbors."[14] Bushman

---

10. Hill, "Joseph Smith," 223–33; on the irregularities that concerned Hill around the reported recovery of the bills, see Hill, 124–26, 153–54, and Larry C. Porter, "Reinventing Mormonism: To Remake or Redo" [review of H. Michael Marquardt and Wesley P. Walters, *Inventing Mormonism: Tradition and the Historical Record* (1994)], *Review of Books on the Book of Mormon* 7, no. 2 (1995), 138–43. On the authenticity of the bills as curated now by The Chenango County Historical Society, Norwich, NY, see Michael Marquardt and Wesley P. Walters, *Inventing Mormonism: Tradition and the Historical Record* (Salt Lake City: Smith Research Associates, 1994), 222–30, and endorsement by the Joseph Smith Papers Project as Fee Bill, ca. Nov. 9, 1826 [State of New York v. JS–A], josephsmithpapers.org.

11. James B. Allen and Glen M. Leonard, *Story of the Latter-day Saints* (Salt Lake City: Deseret Book, 1976), 35–36; Leonard J. Arrington and Davis Bitton, *The Mormon Experience: A History of the Latter-day Saints* (New York: Alfred A. Knopf, 1979), 10–12. On the internal and external target audiences of each (respectively), see Gregory A. Prince, *Leonard Arrington and the Writing of Mormon History* (Salt Lake City: University of Utah and Tanner Trust Fund, 2016), 276–92, 328–31.

12. Donna Hill, *Joseph Smith: The First Mormon* (Garden City, NY: Doubleday, 1977), 62–68.

13. Hill, *Joseph Smith*, 66, 67.

14. Richard L. Bushman, *Joseph Smith and the Beginnings of Mormonism* (Urbana and Chicago: University of Illinois Press, 1984), 72.

highlighted a recently available source as well: a statement from the preliminary manuscript of Joseph Smith's history by his mother about "magic" that had not appeared in any published version.[15] Lucy Mack Smith's statement cautioned that a reader "should not suppose" from her change of theme "that we stopt our labor and went at trying to win the faculty of Abrac drawing Magic circles or sooth saying." Bushman observed, "Lucy's main point was that the Smiths were not as lazy as the [Hurlbut] affidavits claimed ... but she also revealed a knowledge of magic formulas and rituals." Moreover, Bushman opined, the younger Joseph Smith's seer stones and angel visitor of the 1820s would have appeared "to confirm the entire culture of magic" for Joseph Smith Sr. Bushman imagined young Joseph evolving from magic nevertheless. He argued that Joseph Jr. had "misgivings" in helping Stowell search for Spanish treasure, and underwent "a change of perspective."[16] Here Bushman's interpretation assumed a separation between worlds of treasure and religion, and that the young seer abandoned the former for the latter from 1826.

Across these various LDS historian interpretations until 1984, supernatural treasure seeking through a seer stone was largely epiphenomenal to Smith's authentic religious quest. I characterize this limited accommodation as the "scrying as periphery" model. An alternative, if still sympathetic, accommodation of Joseph Smith's religious work and treasure-seeking had emerged simultaneously in an article by Jan Shipps, a non-LDS religious studies scholar. Shipps argued that Smith's treasure seeking was important evidence of his belief in "extra-rational phenomena," and consequently "played an important role in his spiritual development."[17] This proposal anticipated a post-1983 shift in the scholarly interpretive ground. One tragic stimulus was interim acceptance by historians of the forgeries of criminal document dealer and murderer Mark Hofmann, whose fakes began appearing in scholarly works in the early 1980s.

15. Anderson, ed., *Lucy's Book*, 323 and acknowledgement in Richard Lloyd Anderson, "Rodger I. Anderson, *Joseph Smith's New York Reputation Reexamined*," *Review of Books on the Book of Mormon* 3, no. 1 (1991), 77.

16. Bushman, *Joseph Smith*, 72–75. See also Richard L. Bushman, "Treasure-Seeking Then and Now," *Sunstone*, Sep. 1987, 5.

17. Jan Ships, "The Prophet Puzzle: Suggestions Leading toward a More Comprehensive Interpretation of Joseph Smith," *Journal of Mormon History* 1 (1974): 14.

Most sensationally, a fraudulent 1830 Martin Harris letter referred to an "old spirit" guardian of the Book of Mormon "treasure" who "transfigured himself from a white salamander" as Smith sought to recover the plates.[18] The last document, initially deemed plausible by experts, would become known popularly as the Salamander Letter.[19] Intriguingly, among the few skeptics was anti-Mormon evangelical researcher Jerald Tanner, even though the content of the Salamander document was in alignment with his own assumptions about Joseph Smith and treasure-seeking.[20]

Hofmann's forgeries were taken seriously by many scholars otherwise. Most prominently, Alan Taylor, a historian of American culture, utilized them in a 1986 study of late eighteenth to early nineteenth-century treasure seeking in the early republic.[21] This study accepted the Salamander document and another Hofmann "letter" from Joseph Jr. to Josiah Stowell as compatible with pre-1830 northeastern states treasure-seeking accounts.[22] For Taylor, Mormon reticence to discuss the larger topic "perpetuated the anti-Mormons' erroneous presumption that treasure seeking was rare and symptomatic of moral bankruptcy," although he recognized that recent work by Hill and Bushman marked a change. Taylor expanded on this argument in a separate treatment in which supernatural treasure-seeking prepared Joseph Smith for prophethood.[23]

Jan Shipps returned to her earlier developmental interpretation in a landmark 1985 book on Mormonism in which Smith's efforts to find buried treasure with a seer stone "were gradually transformed

---

18. On the context and impact of these documents, see Linda Sillitoe and Allen Roberts, *Salamander: The Story of the Mormon Forgery Murders*, 2nd ed. (Salt Lake City: Signature Books, 1990), and Richard E. Turley, Jr., *Victims: The LDS Church and the Mark Hofmann Case*, updated ed. (N.p.: Anvil & Cross, 2021).

19. Dean C. Jessee, "New Documents and Mormon Beginnings," *BYU Studies* 24, no. 4 (Fall 1984), 397–428; Rhett S. James, "Writing History Must Not Be an Act of 'Magic'," *FARMS Review of Books* 12, no. 2 (2000), 409–11.

20. Jerald Tanner, "Dilemma of a Mormon Critic," *Salt Lake City Messenger* 55 (Jan. 1985): 4–13; see also Jerald Tanner and Sandra Tanner, *Tracking the White Salamander* (Salt Lake City: Utah Lighthouse Ministry, 1993).

21. Alan Taylor, "The Early Republic's Supernatural Economy: Treasure Seeking in the American Northeast, 1780–1830," *American Quarterly* 38, no. 1 (Spring 1986): 6–34.

22. Taylor, "Early Republic's Supernatural Economy," 10–11, 14.

23. Alan Taylor, "Rediscovering the Context of Joseph Smith's Treasure Seeking," *Dialogue: A Journal of Mormon Thought* 19, no. 4 (Winter 1986): 28, 29n10.

into a search for treasure of infinitely greater value." For Shipps, there was "an implicit connection" between these activities.[24] And in 1986, the first chapters of an incomplete church history by late western historian Dale Morgan of Latter-day Saints background (but not personal faith) were published. These presented Morgan's non-supernatural argument that the recovery and "translation" of the Book of Mormon represented a "culmination" of Smith's experiences with seer stones, seeing, and the spirit guardians of ancient treasure.[25]

Influential Latter-day Saints historians responded to these arguments in a much-delayed special issue of *BYU Studies*. The issue was dated fall 1984, but published under copyright and date of 1986. Hofmann's yet-to-be-confirmed forgeries were the backdrop, certainly, but the broader question of the influence of a magic worldview on the early church was the focus.[26] Among these historians, BYU professor Richard Anderson was most skeptical, and argued for a version of the periphery position. Anderson concluded that Lucy's "Faculty of Abrac" and other magic references were "incidental to the deep quest for religion that was their overriding family concern." He also critiqued the idea that treasure seeking had persisted under Joseph Smith's church administration. In particular, Anderson questioned, correctly as it turned out, the authenticity of a purported 1838 treasure revelation from Joseph Smith Jr. (another Hofmann forgery). For Anderson, the "mature spiritual purposes" evident in Smith's later religious work reduced "any treasure seeking to a transitory exploring function for the Prophet's life."[27]

---

24. Jan Shipps, *Mormonism: The Story of a New Religious Tradition* (Urbana and Chicago: University of Illinois Press, 1985), 10–11.

25. John Phillip Walker, ed., *Dale Morgan on Early Mormonism: Correspondence & a New History* (Salt Lake City: Signature Books, 1986), 228–80. Morgan was close to and had corresponded with Fawn Brodie in the 1940s as *No Man Knowns My History* was in preparation. See Walker, 233–43, 263–78.

26. Jessee ("New Documents," 412) observed: "even if the Smith-Harris letters should prove spurious, substantial other early Mormon sources focus on the issues raised." In the same issue, Marvin Hill ("Money-Digging Folklore," 474) argued similarly. The editors' introduction to this special issue advised also that "no matter what the legal verdict on the treasure letters released last year [1985], the underlying historical issues deserve close scrutiny commensurate with the extensive publicity given the problem of Mormon origins," 396).

27. Richard Lloyd Anderson, "The Mature Joseph Smith and Treasure Searching," *BYU Studies* 24, no. 4 (Fall 1984), 508–15, 543, 546.

Other BYU scholars drew from the work of Taylor and Shipps to characterize an evolution in Smith's practice. I term this the "scrying as passage" model. For BYU Smith Institute historian Ronald Walker, the question before scholars now was "no longer if Joseph and his family participated in the cunning arts but the degree and meaning of their activity." He opined that these folk practices were "not an inappropriate precursor to the restoration" in "the idea of personal revelation and the ministry of spirits." The young Smith "transformed himself from 'Joseph, the Palmyra Seer' who likely understood his early religious experiences in one way to the mature 'Joseph the Mormon Prophet' who saw them in quite a different light."[28] Similarly, Marvin Hill shifted from his previously cautious perspective to now identify elements of the recovery of the Book of Mormon record as "very similar to the money digging folklore." Hill suggested that for Smith's early followers, "revealed religion and magic served similar purposes" as "reassuring evidence of the power of God."[29]

Early Mormonism and the Magic World View

Quinn initially accepted expert opinion that the Salamander document was physically and contextually consistent with earlier nineteenth-century origins. But once Hofmann confessed to murder and forgery both in January 1987, Quinn refocused his final research and writing efforts for *Early Mormonism* around the actual historical record. Quinn followed a believing passage model to both clarify and explore the idea that Smith had developed his "inward spirituality" as a "treasure-seer" rather than a "treasure-digger." For the former, "the primary reward was expanding his or her seeric gift," where the seer would absent themselves in general from the actual, physical treasure quest. Quinn observed that this was consistent with early records of the younger Smith's "own lack of involvement" in the actual quest. But for Quinn, Smith was unlike the other seers of 1820s Palmyra as he "soon became remarkable for the manner in which he dramatically expanded the religious dimensions inherent in folk magic." Quinn argued further that "the alleged [1826] court

---

28. Ronald W. Walker, "Joseph Smith: The Palmyra Seer," *BYU Studies* 24, no. 4 (1984): 463, 470.

29. Hill, "Money-Digging," 482, 486.

records portray Smith in a positive light unless, of course, one denies the legitimacy of folk religion."[30]

Early Mormonism also argued that Lucy Mack Smith's passing manuscript observation on magic practices "affirmed" that those activities "were part of the family's religious quest." Moreover, in Quinn's wide-ranging documentation, the "Faculty of Abrac" was confirmed as a "well-known phrase linking magic and divinity." Quinn noted further that Joseph Smith Sr. and Lucy Mack Smith had been accused of these magic practices.[31] By the time he was ready to publish the second edition, Quinn was aware of and cited other accounts showing that Lucy sought seer stones in the 1820s.[32] For Quinn, Lucy's 'Faculty of Abrac' statement also underscored the significance of a ritual dagger and Jupiter talisman that remained in the possession of Hyrum and Joseph Smith respectively.[33]

Quinn's initial research interests in the salamander theme survived into *Early Mormonism* as well, despite his acknowledgment of the letter forgery.[34] Quinn had developed the view that two nineteenth-century accounts of something like a "toad" that appeared when Smith attempted to recover the Book of Mormon plates were more likely to have been a salamander. Quinn cited occult sources that reinforced the symbolism of the mythic, fiery salamander as a more appropriate Book of Mormon guardian spirit. Aware of how this might look, Quinn insisted—in a late footnote to the first edition—that confirmation of the "Harris letter" forgery did not render the salamander argument "any less useful."[35]

---

30. Quinn, *Early Mormonism*, 1st ed., 45, 51, 330n14.
31. Quinn, *Early Mormonism*, 1st ed., 54–56.
32. Quinn, *Early Mormonism*, rev. ed., 42.
33. Quinn, *Early Mormonism*, 1st ed., 57–77.
34. Quinn, *Early Mormonism*, rev. ed., 330n14.
35. Quinn, *Early Mormonism*, 1st ed., 124–33, 33n5. A "frightening toad" was one of the apparitions that might impede digging in the treasure lore of the early republic. Walker, "The Persisting Idea of American Treasure Hunting," *BYU Studies* 24, no. 4 (1984): 432; see also Dan Vogel, ed., *Early Mormon Documents Volume 2* (Salt Lake City: Signature Books, 1998), 67n11). But because the toad of that lore was associated with Satan and "black magic," Quinn argued, it was "unlikely" Joseph Smith Jr. or Sr. would have used the imagery for an amphibian that changed itself into the Book of Mormon guardian. For Quinn, a salamander was the more appropriate image (*Early Mormonism*, 1st ed., 128). The revised edition was less equivocal even about the likelihood that this amphibian was a salamander (*Early Mormonism*, rev. ed., 152, xiii).

Quinn was not alone in considering the salamander sympa-
thetically as a Mormon cultural symbol after January 1987.[36] But
with greater chronological distance and a more sober assessment of
Hofmann's criminality, twenty-first century researchers on Mormon
origins have not endorsed the salamander as a plausible Book of
Mormon guardian. In the words of non-believing Smith biographer
Dan Vogel, "Smith, Chase, and Saunders would have known the difference between a salamander and a toad."[37]

From a documentary perspective, Quinn was on less contentious
ground concerning the curation and use of seer stones and divina-
tory rods with their roots in the popular supernatural materialities of
the early republic. These artifacts and uses followed Mormon leaders
into the early Utah period of church history at least until a more
rationalist view prevailed from the late nineteenth century, Quinn
argued. He also sought to connect practices and beliefs as diverse
as Freemasonry, phrenology, astrology, Cabala, initiatory rites, and
pyramidology to argue, more so than any other believing scholar
had, for multiple "magic" influences on early Mormon society.

Scholarly responses to *Early Mormonism* were mixed. BYU graduate and historian Klaus J. Hansen referred to "the truly stunning
mass of evidence Quinn has assembled in this tour de force."[38] Non-
LDS historians Jon Butler and John L. Brooke relied on Quinn's
evidence in particular in their influential religious history studies
published in 1990 and 1994 respectively. Brooke expressly identified
Early Mormonism as "an invaluable guide and treasure-house of information," even while diverging in interpretation.[39]

LDS historian Bushman was more cautious. He allowed that
"there is evidence here and there of a continuing interest in treasure-
seeking and perhaps a fascination with the ancient lore of magic"

36. Benson Whittle, review of D. Michael Quinn, *Early Mormonism and the Magic World View* (1987), *BYU Studies* 27, no. 4 (Fall 1987), 120–21; John L. Brooke, *The Refiner's Fire: The Making of Mormon Cosmology, 1644–1844* (Cambridge UK: Cambridge University Press, 1994), 300–04; Jon Butler, *Awash In a Sea of Faith: Christianizing the American People* (Cambridge MA: Harvard University Press, 1990), 243–44.

37. Dan Vogel, *Joseph Smith: The Making of a Prophet* (Salt Lake City: Signature Books, 2004), 586n77.

38. Klaus J. Hansen, review of D. Michael Quinn, *Early Mormonism and the Magic World View* (1987), *Church History* 59, no. 1 (March 1990), 110–12.

39. Butler, *Awash*, 243–47; Brooke, *The Refiner's Fire*, xvii.

that "will have to be weighed and entered into the story."[40] More conservative LDS reviewers responded that Quinn's treatments of the possible influence of magic on the prophetic development of Joseph Smith (and Brigham Young to an extent) over-reached and pushed speculative connections and interpretation at the expense of the traditional narrative. Some of these reviews became personal as they called Quinn's motivations and even his faith into question.[41] Quinn's response was equally personal and heated at several places of the revised edition, with his critics dismissed as "polemicists."[42]

Ironically, Quinn's more moderate critics not only accepted his testimony of faith but wondered if Quinn's sympathetic treatment of "magical" practices and ideas displayed a personal acceptance of the "magic world view."[43] Some have recognized also Quinn's belief that God had "literally restored" the "ancient mysteries of deification" through Joseph Smith's Nauvoo endowment ceremony, a belief shared with LDS apologist Hugh Nibley. Brooke went further to infer that these arguments on the part of Nibley and Quinn meant that "the intervening hermetic traditions … were irrelevant."[44] But here Brooke had misread *Early Mormonism*. Quinn in fact had researched and cited those "intervening" traditions more than any ancient history source.[45] For Quinn it seems, those traditions as incorporated into texts that circulated widely in the early republic provided a seedbed of inquiry that would lead to revelation and restoration, as much as seer stones and treasure-seeking had.

The Magic of Diversity: A Reflection on the Legacy of *Early Mormonism*

In the twenty-first century, folklorists Tom Mould and Eric A. Eliason recognize that Quinn's "opus" on magic has informed the

40. Bushman, "Treasure-Seeking," 6.

41. On the last, Quinn cited the "implication" of one reviewer that his statement of belief "was a pretense" (*Early Mormonism*, rev. ed., xii).

42. Quinn, *Early Mormonism*, rev. ed., x–xii.

43. William A. Wilson, review of D. Michael Quinn, "Early Mormonism and the Magic World View (1987), *BYU Studies* 27, no. 4 (Fall 1987): 96; Quinn, *Early Mormonism*, rev. ed., xii.

44. Brooke, *Refiner's Fire*, 301; Michael W. Homer, *Joseph's Temples: The Dynamic Relationship between Freemasonry and Mormonism* (Salt Lake City: University of Utah Press, 2014), 396, 397–98.

45. Quinn, *Early Mormonism*, 1st ed., 184–90.

work of important American religion scholars like Jon Butler and John L. Brooke (cited above), while "profoundly" shaping scholarly understanding of Mormon beginnings and "the cultural backdrop" of the Second Great Awakening. Folklore colleague David Allred adds that *Early Mormonism* constitutes the most "significant" treatment of Mormonism and the occult.[46] The influential Joseph Smith biography by historian Richard L. Bushman also draws on Quinn's research for early Smith family scrying, treasure-seeking, and Book of Mormon origins.[47]

But *Early Mormonism* has had a more limited impact on specialist historical studies of Joseph Smith and the Book of Mormon in the 1820s. A non-believing scholarship has channeled the naturalistic passage model of Dale Morgan.[48] Believing scholars have followed a considerably more modest religious model of scrying as passage, which has become relatively normalized within the twenty-first century church.[49] Indeed, this modest narrative has received quasi-official support through incorporation into the first (2018) volume of the church's most recent approved LDS history, and a topical essay on "treasure seeking" published around the same time on the official "Church History" webpage.[50] In this quasi-official view, the seer stones and associated treasure quest were providential: a training from which Joseph Smith graduated to undertake the sacred and separate work of translation and then prophethood. None

46. Tom Mould and Eric A. Eliason, "The State of Mormon Folklore Studies," *Mormon Studies Review* 1 (2014): 37–38; Allred, "Early Mormon," 188.

47. Bushman, *Rough Stone Rolling*, 572–75 (multiple footnotes).

48. Marquardt and Walters, *Inventing Mormonism*, chs. 4, 5; Vogel, *Joseph Smith*, ch. 4.

49. Mark Ashurst-McGee, "Moroni: Angel or Treasure Guardian?," *Mormon Historical Studies* 2, no. 2 (Fall 2001): 39–75; Terryl L. Givens, *By the Hand of Mormon: The American Scripture that Launched a New World Religion* (New York: Oxford University Press, 2002), 16–19; Dean C. Jessee, Mark Ashurst-McGee, and Richard L. Jensen, eds., *The Joseph Smith Papers: Journals, Volume 1: 1832–1839*, (Salt Lake City: Church Historian's Press, 2008), xix; Richard Lyman Bushman, "Joseph Smith and Money Digging," in *A Reason for Faith: Navigating LDS Doctrine and Church History*, ed. Laura Harris Hales (Provo and Salt Lake City UT: Religious Studies Center, Brigham Young University, and Deseret Book, 2016), 1–5; Larry E. Morris, *A Documentary History of the Book of Mormon* (New York: Oxford University Press, 2019), 7–10.

50. *Saints: The Story of the Church of Jesus Christ in the Latter Days, Volume 1, The Standard of Truth: 1815–1846* (Salt Lake City, Utah: The Church of Jesus Christ of Latter-day Saints, 2018), 21, 25, 31–34; "Treasure Seeking," Church history topics, churchofjesuschrist.org.

of this is far from Quinn's 1987 assertion that the Mormon movement "developed within a particular cultural environment which it rapidly transformed in the process of becoming its own religious tradition."[51] But Quinn was not the first believing scholar to have made this argument, and is not cited in the quasi-official narrative.

Even so, there is a more enduring and novel (if unrealized) value of Quinn's uniquely integrative work for the LDS community. In a review of the first edition of *Early Mormonism*, BYU folklorist William Wilson had critiqued what he perceived to be Quinn's distinction between "the educated or cultivated who abandoned old ways for more rationalistic perspectives and the folk who adhered to the old ways and kept alive the traditional learning of the centuries." For "contemporary folklorists", Wilson argued, "there is no monolithic unchanging group of people called the folk; there are instead many 'folks'" who were "constantly changing."[52]

Sensitive to this critique, Quinn responded that *Early Mormonism* did not exclude elites from the magic worldview. Moreover, one should consider that the "folk religion" of *Early Mormonism* was not, at its core, a static, conservative plank of the rural uneducated "folk" (Quinn's typological sympathies notwithstanding). Rather, Quinn had outlined, with considerable empathy, a dynamic culture history example of the politics of alternative spiritualities. To make the point clear, Quinn added the following text to the second edition: "In the last quarter of the twentieth century, the LDS church also became increasingly authoritarian and obsessed with conformity [including] a complete repudiation of the occult.... Moreover, liberal Mormons are rarely attracted to folk religion and folk magic, despite the latter's anti-institutional emphasis.... That creates a very hostile environment for the survival of esoteric beliefs and behavior. From the perspective of institutional control, that is a victory. From the perspective of human diversity, it is a loss."[53]

Quinn's observations were focused on the historical European "folk" religious views that had nurtured and shaped the church. But this encouragement to understand and respect spiritual diversity

---

51. Quinn, *Early Mormonism*, 1st ed., 227.
52. Wilson, review of Quinn, 100–01.
53. Quinn, *Early Mormonism*, rev. ed., 319, 320.

becomes an important consideration for a world church establishing congregations in Africa, Asia, and western Oceania, and building on long-standing relationships with Indigenous Polynesian and American communities. For example, Indigenous Māori Latter-day Saints have maintained belief in ancestral animal guardians (birds, fishes and dogs) alongside the Anglo-American and Judeo-Christian deities and angels of Mormon culture, despite opposition from North American missionaries and some non-Māori church leaders.[54] Thomas Murphy points also to Indigenous American spiritualities, seers, and scriptures that may help Mormons "better understand not just others but also ourselves."[55] Here, the magic of *Early Mormonism* continues to remind us that religious experience and spiritualities are culturally grounded in the first instance, and as diverse as the many peoples and traditions that have become threads of the global Latter-day Saints movement.

For me, this highlights a persisting lesson of *Early Mormonism*: where a religious society does not allow for or respect diversity in spirituality, it may become unduly conformist and oppressive. The net result, as Quinn observes, is loss.

---

54. Anthropologist Erik Schwimmer reported a Latter-day Saints priesthood meeting from northern Aotearoa in which Māori participants dismissed the suggestion that, "as 'pagan gods,' their ... guardian animals were evil," even while the church regarded them as "idols." They agreed that the influence of these guardians would vanish eventually, but gradually only. Erik Schwimmer, "The Cognitive Aspect of Culture Change," *Journal of the Polynesian Society* 74, no. 2 (June 1965): 165–66, and see also Erik Schwimmer, "Guardian Animals of the Maori," *Journal of the Polynesian Society* 72, no. 4 (Dec. 1963): 397–410. On post-war Anglo-American Latter-day Saints opposition to Māori spirituality followed by a subtle re-accommodation in the later twentieth-century Aotearoa church, see Ian G. Barber, "Lands of Contrast: Latter-day Saint Societies in New Zealand /Aotearoa and Australia," in *The Palgrave Handbook of Global Mormonism*, ed. R. Gordon Shepherd, A. Gary Shepherd, and Ryan T. Cragun (London: Palgrave Macmillan, 2020), 459–65.

55. Thomas W. Murphy, "Other Scriptures: Restoring Voice of Gantowisas to an Open Cannon," in *Essays on American Indian & Mormon History*, ed. P. Jane Hafen and Brenden W. Rensink (Salt Lake City: University of Utah, 2019), 23–40.

Uncovering the "End" of Polygamy: D. Michael Quinn and the Sacred Work of History

CRISTINA ROSETTI

Like many young students of history, D. Michael Quinn's interest in his religion's past began as an undergraduate, in Quinn's case at Brigham Young University. Particularly, his interest in post-Manifesto polygamy began when a fellow student complained about a teacher who said anyone sealed polygamously after the 1890 Manifesto was an adulterer. The student's concern stemmed from his grandfather, a mission president, who was sealed in a post-Manifesto union that was authorized by Joseph F. Smith. Quinn was bothered. Polygamous sealing after the Manifesto was not the history he learned from the devotional works of B. H. Roberts and Joseph Fielding Smith. To find answers, he took to the LDS Church archive where he sought to understand post-Manifesto polygamy, the men who performed the sealings, the subsequent discipline from the church hierarchy, and the families who were silenced from official histories because their marriages were authorized a few years too late.

On August 12, 1974, Quinn, now a graduate student, opened his diary and documented a day spent in the archive of the Church of Jesus Christ of Latter-day Saints. His diary, an archive in itself, revealed the sacred nature of historical inquiry, and the way Quinn felt his work was guided by both rigorous historical methods and a spiritual calling to uncover the past. He wrote:

> In the afternoon I talked with Don Schmidt about the materials in the vault (after I had devoted much silent prayer in the day asking the Lord to guide my words, and open the way for my access).... I asked Don if there was any way I could find out exactly what is in the subject files of the vault, so I wouldn't have to fish around in the dark for what is there.

He readily took me into Earl Olsen's office, picked up the catalogue cards to the vault's contents, and read off the subject titles so that I could indicate which, if any, were of interest to my [dissertation] research on the general authorities. Among the cards he read was the marriage record of 1898–1903, which I said I would like to see in addition to two other items of far less interest to me. He nonchalantly said: "Okay, that's three items. Make up cards requesting them, and give them to me tomorrow."[1]

Quinn intentionally included two documents unrelated to the marriage record in his request so that Schmidt would not recognize the significance of the requested documents. He knew that his request had the potential to alter the historical record. The next day, in answer to his research inquiry and prayer, Quinn received the marriage record he sought from the vault. "When I got the marriage record, I immediately recognized it as containing post-1890 plural marriages performed by Matthias F. Cowley," he recalled.

This record was vital for Quinn's research on post-Manifesto polygamy, and remains a one of the most significant resource for scholars of Mormon plural marriage. It revealed many people sealed by Cowley after the 1890 Manifesto, including fellow apostles Brigham Young Jr., Owen Woodruff, Marriner Merrill, and John W. Taylor. These were in addition to many stake and mission presidents. In my own work, I'm grateful for Quinn's uncovering of the record because it contained the record of future fundamentalist leader Saint Joseph White Musser's third plural sealing to Mary C. Hill in 1902.

Quinn recognized that the Cowley sealing record was a significant historical discovery, and one that would change the trajectory of future research. He wrote:

> I typed extensive notes from the marriage record which contained the record of plural marriages performed for 50 men by Cowley, and a scrap of paper with 2 post-1890 plural marriages performed in 1903 by Apostle Rudger Clawson. I know that Cowley performed more plural marriages than these, so it seems possible that this was an incomplete collation he made, perhaps as required by his arch-opponent Francis M. Lyman.

When I had finished with this record, I turned somewhat indifferently to the second item from the vault, catalogued in Earl Olsen's list

---

1. D. Michael Quinn, diary, Aug. 12, 1974, copy in author's possession. Quinn's diaries are currently being edited and annotated for publication by Bryan Buchanan.

as George F. Richards' appointment book. I had asked for it primarily to act as a filler, so that the marriage record would not be the only item I was seeking.

To my surprize I found that this record book contained a rather detailed summary of the meetings held in connection with the resignations J.W. Taylor and M.F. Cowley submitted in 1905. In none of the available diaries of the Apostles or presidency has more than oblique reference been made to these meetings. Therefore I was profoundly happy and grateful to have stumbled upon this document.

I offered several silent, but heartfelt, prayers to God, thanking Him for giving me access at last to all of the documents apparently in HDC about post-1890 polygamy...

The remaining documents I seek are either in private possession or are in the vaults of the 1st Presidency, or of Joseph Fielding Smith. When it is the Lord's will, I know He will open the way for me to obtain access to the materials."[2]

The above prayer, research, and reflection culminated in one of the most significant pieces of historical writing in the study of post-Manifesto polygamy and Mormon fundamentalism.

Quinn foresaw the significance of his research even before it's publication. He noted that "there is no power on earth that will spare me from excommunication if Mark E. Petersen is alive."[3] Petersen notoriously hated discussion of post-Manifesto polygamy and fundamentalism.[4] The stakes were therefore high for someone whose church membership and faith mattered. But, in the spirit of his mentor and Church Historian Leonard J. Arrington, a history true to the people found in the record mattered at least as much as the institution's reaction to history. The result was the publication of "LDS Church Authority and New Plural Marriages, 1890–1904" in *Dialogue: A Journal of Mormon Thought* in 1985. The "article," which totaled nearly one-hundred pages, raised and answered questions about the ambiguous period between 1890 and 1904. It showed

---

2. Ibid.

3. D. Michael Quinn, "Background and Fallout of My 1985 Article: 'LDS Church Authority and New Plural Marriages, 1890–1904,'" Sunstone, Jan. 31, 2020, sunstone.org.

4. See Gary James Bergera, ed., *Confessions of a Mormon Historian: The Diaries of Leonard J. Arrington, 1971–1997, Volume 2: Centrifugal Forces, 1975–80* (Salt Lake City: Signature Books, 2018), 136–37, 358–61 (Jan. 30, 1976, and Mar. 17, 1977).

in great detail that despite thirteen-and-a-half years and over twenty-four documents denying the continuation of the practice, polygamy continued after the LDS Church's "end" to the controversial marriage system. There is still much for historians to uncover from this period.

In 1909, Saint Joseph White Musser met with the Quorum of the Twelve in the Salt Lake City Temple for a disciplinary hearing.[5] Musser was a polygamist who had been sealed to his second wife under the sealing authority of Matthias F. Cowley in 1902. We have this record because of Quinn. During the meeting, Musser met with several men who themselves either solemnized plural marriages or married plural wives after the Manifesto. Before learning this from Musser's diaries, which remain restricted in the Church Historical Department, I knew the names of these men from Quinn's work: John Henry Smith, Rudger Clawson, Heber J. Grant, and Anthony W. Ivins. In his longest journal entry to date, Musser gave a detailed overview of the two-hour interaction where he was the "object of inquisition, to get information regarding the practice of Plural Marriage since the discontinuance thereof by the church."[6] Musser recounted:

> My own feelings are these: That the investigation along the lines it is being carried out, is unwarranted. That the Quorum is not united, and that such actions as these will tend to lose them their influence among the Saints. Bro. Grant said they were going to cut Bro. Higgs off the Church, and his tone and manner was vindictive. My impressions were that the brethren are not activated by the proper spirit.... I can't understand the attitude of some of my brethren, but am willing to leave all for final working out of our God, seeking to be an humble instrument in his hands at all times in doing good.[7]

The lack of uniform policy was only exacerbated by Musser's suspicion that further discipline would happen for his stake president, William H. Smart, who was similarly an unrepentant polygamist.

---

5. While Musser's civil documents omit "Saint," it was the name given at his blessing and remains on some Church records. The name given at his blessing was noted during the 2022 annual meeting of the Mormon History Association by David G. Watson, the man who currently succeeds Musser in the Apostolic United Brethren.

6. Joseph White Musser, Journal, July 22, 1909, in Joseph White Musser Journals, 1895–1911, MS 1862, LDS Church History Library. Photocopy in author's possession.

7. Ibid.

When Musser noted the quorum was not united, he spoke of the stark reality that the Quorum of the Twelve, and the leadership of the church generally, was divided over plural marriage. This was most clearly manifest by the resignation of Matthias Cowley and John W. Taylor, who were found "out of harmony" with the quorum only three years before Musser's meeting, and therefore removed from their apostleships. Yet contrary to what some have written about Musser's life, Musser's 1909 meeting did not result in formal church discipline despite his plural sealings in 1902 and 1907.

Quinn's work affirmed what many knew from family keepsakes and genealogical records. Polygamy after the Manifesto was not relegated to the "other" Mormons, the "bad" religious like Lorin C. Woolley and his Council of Friends.[8] However, as the church sought to "convince a doubting nation" about the end of polygamy, as one author put it, a sacrifice was required.[9] In Quinn's words, "Apostles Taylor and Cowley may have been scapegoats to satisfy anti-Mormons and to protect the Church."[10] These were not rogue men—they were men whose stories were disappeared into an archival record. Answering the historical questions he first encountered as an undergraduate student, Quinn recognized that "the descendants of authorized post-Manifesto polygamists have suffered from the Church's effort to maintain consistency by branding these marriages unauthorized."[11] Of course, other post-Manifesto plural marriages were unauthorized. But many were. Quinn's research uncovered hundreds of people who were sealed by "correct" authority following the First and Second Manifestos.

Everyone had an opinion about Quinn's article. For scholars of Mormon fundamentalism, the record of Matthias Cowley and others made tangible the ambiguous period after the Manifestos. For families of the proto-fundamentalists, the history was a vindication,

---

8. For more on the differentiation between "good" and "bad" religion, as it relates to the nation see Peter Coviello, *Make Yourselves Gods: Mormonism and the Unfinished Business of American Secularism* (Chicago: University of Chicago Press, 2019).

9. Marianne T. Watson, "Short Creek: 'A Refuge for the Saints,'" *Dialogue: A Journal of Mormon Thought* 36, no. 1 (Spring 2003): 75.

10. D. Michael Quinn, "LDS Church Authority and New Plural Marriages, 1890–1904," *Dialogue: A Journal of Mormon Thought* 18, no. 1 (Spring 1985): 104.

11. Ibid., 104–05.

a reckoning that their families were valid. Some former members of the church, conversely, called it an "expose," and many faithful Latter-day Saints struggled with the revealed history. Some still struggle. All of these responses were realities that Quinn knew, because he grappled with them all. He brought empathy to the telling of history. He explained, "The resulting situation caused significant segments of the Mormon Church to function in 'cognitive dissonance' for prolonged periods of time. We can ignore the past; we can even deny it; but we cannot escape its intrusion upon out faithful history.... History is what we are able to discover of the past; historical fantasy is what we wish had occurred."[12] The past was not something to be silenced or disappeared. God commanded the Saints to keep a record, with no qualifications. As Arrington said to his research assistants, including Quinn, the record revealed a people marked by the best of humanity and the warts and scars of real people. The history needed to be told "warts and all."[13]

The disappearance of Cowley's sealings, a perceived wart on the past, from the official record was not only an absence, but an effective silence. Silences are more powerful than absences in the telling of history because they are overt exercises of power. Quinn knew this well. In framing Cowley and Taylor as scapegoats in Mormonism's path toward secularity, he made loud a historic silence. Quinn's work found entire histories in the gaps made through silence. People, families, and entire communities were found in Cowley's record book. When Quinn broke open the records of 1,000 post-Manifesto sealings, he did not simply reveal a piece of data. He opened the records of people bound for eternity by priesthood and belief.

In *Phantoms of Remembrance*, Patrick J. Geary writes of the haunting presence of the dead as the primary concern of history.[14] He questioned whether our ghosts are those preserved in the historical record or the individual who maintains the record. Behind this question is the problem of who creates history and whether there is an intention in creating a specific version of the past. History is made,

---

12. Ibid., 105.

13. Bergera, *Confessions of a Mormon Historian*, 116 (Nov. 18, 1975).

14. See Patrick J. Geary, *Phantoms of Remembrance: Memory and Oblivion at the End of the First Millennium* (Princeton: Princeton University Press, 1994).

UNCOVERING THE "END" OF POLYGAMY

it is not a given, and it is always made by a haunted people. Quinn's work exemplified the scholar's inseparable connection to this reality. For Quinn, history was a sacred practice. He ended his article on post-Manifesto polygamy with a testimony that despite the history, he maintained that "Jesus the Christ restored the Church with all its authority, exalting doctrine, and ordinances to the earth through living prophets."[15] History was deeply connected to who he was, and a faith that made the redemption of the dead part of its mission. As Lindsay Hansen Park has discussed in conversations about her own work, history is a Mormon practice because it invokes the fourth mission of the Church of Jesus Christ of Latter-day Saints: redeeming the dead. Through his research on Cowley, Taylor, Woolley, and others, Quinn sought the fulfillment of this mission. He brought Cowley and his companions up from the dust and redeemed their history.

Building on Quinn's foundational archival work, historians have pieced together the complexity that arose from the Church's long end to polygamy. Ken Driggs's "After the Manifesto: Modern Polygamy and Fundamentalist Mormons (*Journal of Church and State* 32, no. 2 [Spring 1990]) and "Twentieth-Century Polygamy and Fundamentalist Mormons in Southern Utah" (*Dialogue: A Journal of Moron Thought* 24, no. 4 [Winter 1991]), and Brian Hale's *Modern Polygamy and Mormon Fundamentalism: The Generations after the Manifesto* offered readers a concise overview of the major moments in post-Manifesto polygamy and the way that Mormon fundamentalism was shaped by the church's handling of polygamy in the twentieth century. Craig Foster and Newell Bringhurst's *The Persistence of Polygamy* series (John Whitmer Books, 2005–06), as well as Foster and Marianne Watson's *American Polygamy: The History of Fundamentalist Mormon* (The History Press, 2019), similarly demonstrates the way that the "end" of LDS polygamy was not the end of the practice, but the beginning of diverse movements that stemmed from Joseph Smith's original marriage revelations. Finally, Martha Bradley-Evans's *Kidnapped from that Land* (University of Utah Press, 1993) and Janet Bennion's body of work on Mormon fundamentalism made use of Quinn's research into post-Manifesto

---

15. Quinn, "LDS Church Authority," 105.

polygamy and expanded on the history of the "other" Mormons whose lives were impacted by the way the LDS Church sought to separate itself form its supposed "apostates." Contemporarily, myself and others have looked to Quinn's archival findings as a way to shape ethnographic accounts of fundamentalist Mormons, taking seriously their history and the way the period between 1890 and 1922 lays the foundation for the lived experience of Mormon polygamy in the twenty-first century.

Quinn ended his article by noting that men like John W. Woolley, Samuel Eastman, and Judson Tolman solemnized plural marriages without the First Presidency. They were part of the pesky unauthorized plural sealings that raised more questions about the "end" of polygamy and the Mormons who separated from the LDS Church. Joseph Musser's own third marriage was solemnized in his home by Tolman in 1907. Prior to his death, Quinn planned a book that expanded his work on post-manifesto polygamy to 1925. His plan was to focus only on LDS marriages, however, and not wade into the waters of those who split from the institutional church. In his words, he did not want to be "one of those polemical writers."[16] His fidelity to history's sacred cause was absolute.

But, speaking to these proto-fundamentalist marriages, Quinn closed by telling readers that the rest of the story remains to be told. This began with the groundbreaking work of Brian Hales, Craig Foster, Marianne Watson, Ken Driggs, and Martha S. Bradley. I am hopeful that the many of us who write about these "other" sealings and "other" Mormons continue to tell the story that remained to be told, always pointing back to Quinn and the foundation he laid. Quinn was, and is, foundational to the literature on post-Manifesto polygamy. More than simply his work, he, as a scholar and faithful Mormon, was part of the historiography. May he live eternal in our field.

---

16. Quinn, "Background and Fallout."

Documenting Gender and Sexuality in Mormonism: D. Michael Quinn, LGBTQ Historiography, and Making Religion Matter

K. MOHRMAN

I begin this meditation on D. Michael Quinn's place within and influence on the historiography of gender and sexuality in Mormonism with an anecdote about my one and only interaction—or what is more accurately described as an *almost* interaction—with Quinn himself. Starting with this briefly sketched scene serves as a kind of self-positioning, a practice critical for feminist and queer studies scholars such as myself, and one that Quinn himself regarded as imperative. But I also begin with this story because it functions as a pertinent metaphor for what it means to bring Mormon studies into conversation with outside fields, disciplines, and critical theoretical frameworks, and for what, at times, can be more difficult: for those fields, disciplines, and theories to take Mormonism specifically, and religion generally, seriously. Hopefully this examination, albeit brief, of Quinn's legacy within gender and sexuality studies encourages scholars of Mormonism to, like Quinn himself, address questions and engage theories that have been largely ignored.

I found myself in the summer of 2012 having just completed the first year of my PhD program and sitting in the University of Utah's J. Willard Marriott Library Special Collections reading room. A white, queer, non-Mormon woman who had grown up in Mormon-dominated Utah and who was training in a post-nationalist American studies program that had little-to-no focus on religion, I was attempting to find my way through what it meant to study queerness in Utah. I was therefore visiting several archives in Salt Lake City that summer looking for material related to the practice, conceptualization, and management of non-normative sex in nineteenth-century Utah. In hindsight, this focus was inevitably channeled toward an examination of how the Church of Jesus Christ of Latter-day Saints had conceptualized and handled questions of same-sex sex and sexuality.

My research unavoidably veered in this direction largely because the guiding light that kept me from stumbling around in the pro-verbial dark of the archives was the assiduously and painstakingly detailed documentation of primary sources undertaken by Quinn in *Same-Sex Dynamics among Nineteenth-Century Americans: A Mormon Example.* What has been frequently characterized as the overdocu-mentation of his text is an aspect that several reviewers, specifically reviewers outside of Mormon studies, deemed curious and perhaps even a detraction from Quinn's thesis. Indeed, one reviewer high-lighted that over half of the 487-page book was devoted to footnotes and an appendix, contending that such "overdocumentation, in my opinion, is unnecessary; the argument is persuasive without listing thirty or forty sources for a single point."[1]

However, those familiar with both the church's twentieth-cen-tury attitude toward LGBTQ people, as well as how that attitude has affected Mormon studies, understand why Quinn felt it was necessary to complete such an exhaustive documentation given its religious, cultural, academic, and political context. Moreover, his de-tailed documentation allows researchers, fledging (as I was at the time) or practiced, to follow through on their own related lines of investigation—something I could not have done at the time even with digital access. It is also a practice I have striven to emulate in my own book, *Exceptionally Queer: Mormon Peculiarity and U.S. Nation-alism.* This is not to promote or privilege historical methods that put a premium on written, archival sources, since that all too easily erases the voices, experiences, and knowledges of a variety of marginalized folks, especially women and LGBTQ people of color.[2] Rather, it is to acknowledge the political realities of producing such scholarship and

    1. Stephen J. Stein, review of *Same-Sex Dynamics among Nineteenth-Century Ameri-cans: A Mormon Example* by D. Michael Quinn," *Church History* 77, no. 2 (June 1998): 422.
    2. Elise Boxer et al., "Roundtable Discussion: Challenging Mormon Race Scholar-ship," *Journal of Mormon History* 41, no. 3 (July 2015): 258–81.

to encourage reflection on what sources, as opposed to the process of documentation itself, are regarded as "evidence" in the first place.

Sitting at my designated table that August afternoon in the university library, combing through boxes and folders of material with his footnotes as my guide, I looked up to see Quinn himself walking to the archivist's desk to exchange boxes. To put it bluntly, and embarrassingly, I was star-struck. There I was, conducting my own research under Quinn's guidance, unknown to him, and there he was, conducting his own research. I sat there amazed at seeing an academic celebrity of Mormon studies, something that my peers in the American Studies Department at the University of Minnesota would have never understood since they consistently asked me "Why are you studying Mormonism?" But I was too afraid to get up and introduce myself. Regrettably, I never did get up, but rather remained conspicuously aware of his presence for the rest of that afternoon, as a marked up and dogeared copy of his book lay hidden in my bag.

As much as I was star struck by Quinn, and I truly was since there was someone who had written one of the only major works on gay and lesbian Mormon history at the time, I was also critical of some of his theoretical choices in *Same-Sex Dynamics*. I was amazed someone had done this work, but I was also disappointed that he had not gone further in his analysis. Quinn was clearly aware of and engaged in what were then, in the early 1990s, timely academic discussions around what is meant to research and write gay and lesbian history; in debates over what exactly constituted the history of sexuality; and in dialogues about what it meant to contend that sexuality is socially constructed. This was encapsulated in his statement in the introduction to *Same-Sex Dynamics* that "even my use of 'sexuality' is a product of my culture," as well as his citation of scholars such as Carol Vance, Johnathan Ned Katz, Jeffery Weeks, and David Halperin, among others. However, he nevertheless retained a somewhat uncritical attachment to both sexuality and gender as concepts.

While Quinn's work was clearly attentive to what Weeks called sexuality's relationship to "the working[s] of power in contemporary society," specifically to how conceptualizations of sexuality were structured by religious institutions and leaders and how those changed over time, Quinn was surprisingly inattentive to sexuality's relationship to other social categories including class, gender, and most importantly, in my estimation, race.[3] This is reflected in another reviewer's disappointment with what he called Quinn's "simplistic" explanation that the major change in the church's relatively tolerant attitudes toward homosexuality between the nineteenth and twentieth centuries was a result of "the rise of a leadership born in the early twentieth century," a conclusion that left "almost any informed reader unsatisfied."[4] While other scholars have since stepped in to offer other explanations for this change in attitude and approach, myself and Taylor Petrey included, at the time I was left unsatisfied as well, sensing that this change could not be fully explained without an intersectional approach.[5]

I do not include a discussion of my criticism of Quinn's text just for the sake of criticism, nor do I want to hold Quinn to anachronistic standards given the developments in gender and sexuality studies in the twenty-six years since the publication of *Same-Sex Dynamics*. To do so would be both unfair and ludicrous. Rather, I do so because I think part of what held me back from talking to Quinn that day in the archives was my critique of his work, when that should have done just the opposite: driven me to engage him.

This regret feeds directly into a series of questions with which I have grappled since the beginning of my graduate studies and have remained guiding forces for me as an interdisciplinary scholar who is committed to feminist, queer, and other kinds of critical theory, as well as one who is also located at the intersections of Mormon, American, religious, ethnic, gender, and sexuality studies. Why isn't religion, specifically Mormonism in this case, taken seriously beyond religious studies in general, and American religious history in particular? How can religion be conceptualized and fully engaged, not just as "a stultifying, oppressive institution of a [homophobic], sexist

---

3. Jeffrey Weeks, *Sexuality*, 2nd ed. (New York: Routledge, 1986), 34.
4. Benson Tong, review of *Same-Sex Dynamics among Nineteenth-Century Americans: A Mormon Example* by D. Michael Quinn," *Western Historical Quarterly* 28, no. 3 (Autumn 1997): 409.
5. Taylor Petrey, *Tabernacles of Clay: Sexuality and Gender in Modern Mormonism* (Chapel Hill: University of North Carolina Press, 2020).

social order"?[6] On the flip side, how can Mormon studies more deeply and consistently engage the theoretical frameworks, developments, and insights of gender, sexuality, and ethnic studies?

A survey of the current state of the field in gender and sexuality studies suggests that despite contributions like Quinn's and other feminist Mormon studies work, these dynamics are still strongly at play, repeating patterns that have long been in place and reinforcing the walls between fields. One need look no further than the recently published *Keywords for Gender and Sexuality Studies*, which was released in November 2021 by NYU Press. In the introduction to the text written by "The Keywords Feminist Editorial Collective," which was made up of some of today's top scholars in these fields, they describe how they selected which terms would appear in the volume. They explain that in reaching out to "fellow teachers, activists, and thinkers at the 2019 National Women's Studies Association conference in San Francisco," they tested their "intuitions about what to include and how."[7] The response the editorial collective received prompted them to add six more terms to the volume, including *religion*. This demonstrates that the concept was not originally regarded as essential, although it is unclear if they "had either not thought of or eliminated [religion] from the earlier list"; either way the term's almost absence and its eventual inclusion as a result of feminist scholarly praxis (i.e., the editorial collective asking for input from the broader gender and sexuality studies scholarly community) is significant.[8]

In the resulting *Keywords* entry for "religion," Tazeen M. Ali, a scholar of religion, politics, and gender, succinctly explains how religion is still "either rendered suspect in the broader struggle for gender justice or otherwise overlooked as a productive category of inquiry by feminist and queer academics and activists alike."[9] This,

---

6. Melissa Wilcox, "Outlaws or In-Laws? Queer Theory, LGBT Studies, and Religious Studies," in *LGBT Studies and Queer Theory: New Conflicts, Collaborations, and Contested Terrain*, ed. Karen E. Lovaas, John P. Elia, and Gust A. Yep (Binghamton, N.Y.: Harrington Park Press, 2006), 94.

7. The Keywords Feminist Editorial Collective, "Introduction," *Keywords for Gender and Sexuality Studies* (New York: New York University Press, 2021), 6–7.

8. Ibid., 7.

9. Tazeen M. Ali, "Religion" in *Keywords for Gender*, 184.

ironically enough given feminist and queer theory's orientations and commitments, results from the unmarked and still powerful hold of a "western liberal system" that prizes a constellation of relationally defined values including "individualism, freedom, and capitalism."[10] This ideological influence continues to go largely unmarked when it comes to gender and sexuality studies scholars' engagement (or lack thereof) with religion, despite major critiques from within the field, such as Jasbir Puar's now classic *Terrorist Assemblages: Homonationalism in Queer Times* and Evren Savci's more recently published *Queer in Translation: Sexual Politics Under Neoliberal Islam.*[11]

Just as telling, however, is that despite three decades of debate over the definition and goals of feminism and the problems with centering "woman" and "gay" as the primary objects of study in gender and sexuality studies, the now-common conceptualizations of gender and sexuality, "through the prisms of racialization, coloniality, nation, and class" have yet to be widely taken up in Mormon studies.[12] Indeed, many of the critiques, insights, and contributions of gender and sexuality studies over the last thirty-odd years, which are elsewhere taken for granted, cannot yet be assumed in a Mormon studies context.

This disciplinary distance is revealing. Some of these critiques, insights, and contributions include, as the *Keywords* editorial collective reminds us, that the appropriation of feminism by white liberalism has occurred "without acknowledging how race, colonialism, political economy, gender, and other structural inequalities differentiate women's experiences"; that "feminist political concerns have often emerged in political and intellectual spaces not explicitly named or framed as feminist because they did not always foreground 'woman' as a primary subject"; that "gender binarisms, such as the one that upholds biological womanhood as an essential category, are themselves in league with the project of white supremacy, which reserves normative gender identity for white subjects"; and finally, that

---

10. Ibid.

11. Jasbir Puar, *Terrorist Assemblages: Homonationalism in Queer Times* (Durham, NC: Duke University Press, 2007), and Evren Savci, *Queer in Translation: Sexual Politics under Neoliberal Islam* (Durham, NC: Duke University Press, 2021).

12. Keywords Feminist Editorial Collective, "Introduction," 2.

intersectionality as a critical social theory, among other analyses, interpretations, and contributions in gender and sexuality studies.[13]

This is not to ignore the important and groundbreaking work of many Mormon studies scholars that seek to bring these fields, disciplines, and theoretical frameworks into conversation with one another. Take for example the work of Sujey Vega on intersectionality, mujerista theology, and LDS Latina experiences, or Amanda Hendrix-Komoto on LDS theology, settler colonialism, and how nineteenth-century processes of racialization intersect with sexuality. Similar work includes Elise Boxer's on Mormon settler colonialism and racial identity, Chiung Hwang Chen and Ethan Yorgason's on intersectionality as an important framework for Mormon studies, anthologies such as Gina Colvin and Joanna Brooks's edited collection *Decolonizing Mormonism*, and, of course, historical scholarship which builds directly off Quinn's legacy, such as Taylor Petrey and Neil J. Young's work on the ways the church's approach to same-sex sexuality and gender roles have changed over time. While these are not the only examples—there is indeed exciting work coming from the latest generation of Mormon studies scholars—there is much room left to apply critical ethnic, feminist, and queer theoretical approaches to the broader Mormon studies project.[14]

---

13. Ibid., 2–3.

14. Sujey Vega, "Mujerista Theology" in *The Routledge Handbook on Mormonism and Gender*, ed. Taylor Petrey and Amy Hoyt (New York: Routledge, 2020), 598–607; Amanda Hendrix-Komoto, *Imperial Zions: Religion, Race, and Family in the American West and the Pacific* (Lincoln: University of Nebraska Press, 2022); Elise Boxer, "'The Lamanites Shall Blossom as the Rose': The Indian Student Placement Program, Mormon Whiteness, and Indigenous Identity," *Journal of Mormon History* 41, no. 4 (2015): 132–76; Elise Boxer, "The Book of Mormon as Mormon Settler Colonialism," in *Essays on American Indians and Mormon History*, ed. Brenden Rensick and P. Jane Hafen (Salt Lake City: University of Utah Press, 2019); Chiung Hwang Chen and Ethan Yorgason, "Intersectionality," in *Routledge Handbook of Mormonism and Gender*; Gina Colvin and Joanna Brooks, eds., *Decolonizing Mormonism: Approaching a Postcolonial Zion* (Salt Lake City: University of Utah Press, 2018); Petrey, *Tabernacles of Clay*; Neil J. Young, "Fascinating and Happy: Mormon Women, the LDS Church, and the Politics of Sexual Conservatism," in *Devotions and Desires: Histories of Religion and Sexuality in the Twentieth Century United States*, ed. Gillian Frank, Bethany Moreton, and Heather White (Chapel Hill: University of North Carolina Press, 2018); Neil J. Young, "Mormons and Same-Sex Marriage: From ERA to Prop 8," in *Out of Obscurity: Mormonism Since 1945*, ed. John Turner and Patrick Mason (New York: Oxford University Press, 2016); and Neil J. Young, "'The ERA Is a Moral Issue': The Mormon Church, LDS Women, and the Defeat of the Equal Rights Amendment," *American Quarterly* 59, no. 3 (Sep. 2007): 623–44.

As scholars of Mormonism continue to move toward a deeper engagement with gender and sexuality studies, its methods, theoretical frameworks, and commitment to praxis, we are beginning to uncover the myriad ways that Mormonism is, alongside other religious traditions and institutions, central and not peripheral to major social and political events, both historically and contemporaneously. However, I want to caution scholars engaging gender and sexuality in Mormon studies to not limit foci to certain topics or in ways that have most usually been engaged and applied. This includes polygamy, same-sex sexuality, mainstream Mormon feminism, hegemonic Western ideas of gendered authority in theology and institutions, mixed sexuality marriages, as well as an assumed "natural" opposition between LGBTQ rights and religious freedom. While these topics are unavoidable and important, the tendency to focus in these areas and in these ways can have the unintended, but nonetheless detrimental, effect of reifying preconceptions about Mormonism, as well as typical binaries that have structured approaches to gender and sexuality in modern Western thought (e.g., man versus woman, homosexual versus heterosexual, religious versus secular, etc.).

It makes sense that topics like nineteenth-century polygamy and, increasingly, the church's twentieth-century heterosexist and homophobic views and policies, have been the two main foci of research thus far, especially in the history of sexuality. But what about interracial sex and marriage? What about dating, sex work, pornography, or other sexual cultures outside of marriage? What about views and theories of non-procreative sex and pleasure? What about trans and non-binary people and experiences, especially pertinent given the current anti-trans legislative backlash across the country and in Utah specifically? What about Mormon feminisms that don't center white, American, and/or cisgender women? How do any of these questions change when we don't assume a U.S.-centric Mormonism?

Possibilities abound for such research. For instance, how have the church's policies on gender and sexuality traveled with missionaries and other church representatives as the religion has expanded globally? How have those policies come into contact with, challenged, or changed local sexual and gender cultures? Has Mormon missionizing significantly collided with the policing or securitization of national borders as those processes occur through the racially charged registers of gender and sexuality? Given the ways that Mormonism's relationship to sexuality and gender has consistently produced racial meanings, categories, and knowledges used to bolster US settler colonialism and imperial governance, it is imperative that scholars continue to ask these and other questions with attention to the transnational context in which Mormonism has always existed.

These are but a few of the directions open to future scholars of Mormonism and the history of sexuality and gender. Regardless of the questions asked or directions taken, scholars can and should learn from both Quinn's successes and shortcomings in order to, as the *Keywords* editorial collective encourages, embrace the "opportunity to deepen analyses of the relationships among race, gender, sexuality, nation, ability, and political economy as foregrounded in the rich history of justice-oriented intersectional movements," and to "center scholarship enacting the analyses [of] Black, Indigenous, and woman of color feminisms; transnational feminisms; queer of color critique; trans, disability, and fat studies; feminist science studies; and critiques of the state, law, detention centers, and prisons that emerge from within queer and woman of color justice movements."[15] Forever indebted to Quinn's legacy and with such exciting paths forward, there is much to look forward to in Mormon studies.

---

15. Keywords Feminist Editorial Collective, "Introduction," 5.

Polygamy and Revelation in Magical Mormonism: Four Peepstone Bride Narratives

MILLIE TULLIS

"Have you heard the story of the peepstone brides?" a Preston, Idaho, attorney asks in Austin and Alta Fife's landmark study of Mormon folklore, *Saints of Sage and Saddle*.[1] He describes how "Brother Samuel Rose Parkinson" went to see a man with a peepstone in Kaysville, Utah, about his lost mules. In those days, "there were a lot of stories round about to the effect that people had found ... all kinds of things by looking in it." Looking into the peepstone, the man located Samuel's mules nearby. He then invited Samuel "to look too: there were only a few people, he explained, that could see anything in the large opaque stone but he always let them try to satisfy their curiosity." Looking into the peepstone, Samuel saw the mules' location himself. He then asked his wife if there was anything she would "like to look in the peepstone and see about?"

> Well, there were a lot of men who were taking plural wives about that time and so Sam's wife says: "Yes! Look in and see if you kin find something out about your other wives—if you are going to have any more." So Sam takes another look and there he sees two beautiful girls dressed exactly alike and standing arm in arm. He pulled his head away and blushed as red as a beet so his wife grabs the stone and takes a good look.[2]

Samuel's wife sees the same girls in the peepstone. As they drive home Samuel asked her, "If you ever see those two girls will you let me marry them?"[3] She replied, "Yes ... but you'll never see them."

---

1. Austin Fife and Alta Fife, *Saints of Sage and Saddle: Folklore Among the Mormons* (Bloomington: Indiana University Press, 1956), 166. The following quotations are from the same Fife version.
2. Ibid., 166–7.
3. Ibid., 167.

Five years later, Samuel and his wife had settled in Franklin, Idaho, in Northern Cache Valley. In Franklin, Samuel "became the first counselor to the bishop" and opened a grist mill with Thomas Smart. As Samuel was "opening Sunday school" one Sunday, "he looked down to the back of the meeting house and there he saw two girls enter—dressed alike and arm-in-arm as he had seen them in the peepstone." The two "girls" were the daughters of his business partner, Thomas Smart. After church, Samuel asked his wife, "Who did Tom's girls make you think of today in church?" She "confessed" that "they looked exactly like the girls we saw in the peepstone." The Fife's account of this story simply concludes: "That is how Tom Smart's daughters became the plural wives of Samuel Parkinson."

The Fifes published this story in *Saints of Sage and Saddle* without commentary or analysis, and they did not publish alternative versions. Yet, while the Fife's presented the account as being a direct quote from the attorney himself, their sources reveal this story was actually a composite of two sources. In fact, the Fifes pulled more heavily from a 1940 family narrative written by Luella P. Cowley than the 1946 interview they had with the Preston attorney, Arthur W. Hart. In combining these stories, the Fifes made several significant changes. This paper will consider the Fife's version of this Mormon folklore narrative, as well as Cowley and Hart's versions, in conversation with a version from Parkinson descendant Carma L. Sandberg written in 1972. Although there are clear similarities between these stories—a peepstone prompts a vision of Samuel's future wives, two young women who are dressed alike, and the vision is confirmed when he sees them at Church—there are also meaningful variations between them. Examining these variations illuminates how the intersections of gender, divine revelation, spiritual authority, magical practices, and polygamy are negotiated by the storytellers who sought to trivialize or sanctify their narratives at different points throughout the twentieth century.

Mormon Folklore

As Eric A. Eliason established, the field of folklore has had a long and fruitful engagement with Mormon studies and history.[4] However,

---

4. Eric A. Eliason, "Seer Stones, Salamanders, and Early Mormon 'Folk Magic' in the Light of Folklore Studies and Bible Scholarship," *BYU Studies Quarterly* 55, no. 1

while "historians inside and outside of Mormonism have long used 'folk' as a synonym for 'superstitious' ... professional folklorists define folklore not by its respectability or truth value but by its means of transmission—*face-to-face, intimate, and sometimes unofficial within small groups.*"[5] Folklore studies therefore turns its gaze to the informal practices, traditions, and stories that permeate groups' sense of self. Folklore, in other words, takes the informal, often unacknowledged culture that shapes groups and renders this significant knowledge visible. The coupling between history and folklore is a fruitful one as it allows scholars to consider the often-overlooked expressions of a group's culture within the broader context of that group's history.

These "peepstone bride" stories follow the same basic narrative structure, yet each version was recounted or written from different speakers at various points in the twentieth century. While the Fifes were conducting research and writing for an academic audience, Hart was passing on a local story he'd heard from a friend. Cowley and Sandberg were writing family stories that had been passed to them orally and were likely heard many times. While transcribing or writing these stories down gives them a permanence on the page, oral stories are always in flux—they are shaped by memory and time, but also by the speaker, the audience, and the performance context of the storytelling event.[6] When an oral story is performed, "each new audience gets a unique, contextually specific version, and each new teller is as much the rightful 'owner' as the next."[7] Our knowledge

---

(2016): 73–93. For the fruits of this engagement see: Christopher Blythe, *Terrible Revolution: Latter-Day Saints and the American Apocalypse* (New York: Oxford University Press, 2022); Margaret Brady, *Mormon Healer & Folk Poet: Mary Susannah Fowler's Life of 'Unselfish Usefulness'* (Logan: Utah State University Press, 2000); Eric A. Eliason and Tom Mould, eds., *Latter-day Lore: Mormon Folklore Studies* (Salt Lake City: University of Utah Press, 2013); Tom Mould and Eric A. Eliason, "The State of Mormon Folklore Studies," *Mormon Studies Review* 1 (2014): 29–51; W. Paul Reeve and Michael Scott Van Wagenen, *Between Pulpit and Pew: The Supernatural World in Mormon History and Folklore* (Logan: Utah State University Press, 2011).

5. Eliason, "Seer Stones," 75. Emphasis mine.

6. Alan Dundes, "Text, Texture, and Context" in *Interpreting Folklore*, ed. Alan Dundes (Bloomington: Indiana University Press, 1980); Dan Ben-Amos, "Toward a Definition of Folklore in Context," *The Journal of American Folklore* 84, no. 331 (1971): 3–15.

7. Lynne S. McNeill, *Folklore Rules: A Fun, Quick, and Useful Introduction to the Field of Academic Folklore Studies* (Logan: Utah State University Press, 2013), 8.

about these storytelling events are limited, but we can glean some contextual insight from the speakers and their likely audiences.

The Fifes were members of the Mormon community they studied, but they were also scholars. With the publication of *Saints of Sage and Saddle*, they aimed to share some of the stories they collected from their community with the broader academic world of folklorists. Cowley, publishing this story in *Heart Throbs of the West* in 1940, was primarily writing for a Mormon audience, and likely a largely female one. Born in 1870, Cowley observed the shifting policies of the church surrounding the practice of polygamy firsthand.[8] She was the daughter Maria Smart, Samuel's third wife, and watched her father serve in the Old Idaho Penitentiary for unlawful cohabitation.[9] Moreover, her husband, Matthias F. Cowley, was removed from his position as a church apostle in 1905 because he continued performing post-manifesto plural marriages.[10] Luella was the third of his five wives.

Like Matthias F. Cowley, Arthur W. Hart was also a post-manifesto polygamist.[11] Hart married his first wife, Ada Doney Lowe, in 1900. Cowley performed the marriage between Hart and his second wife, Evadyna Henderson, in 1903.[12] However, like the Fife's account, this story was not a family one for Hart. He may have considered it an amusing local tale, spiritual anecdote, neighborhood gossip, or a combination of these. As he says at the beginning of his story, he certainly saw it as a "comical" one.[13]

Sandberg wrote to the Fifes almost two decades after the first publication of *Saints of Sage and Saddle*, and almost three decades

8. "Luella Smart Parkinson," FamilySearch (Person ID: KWCH-JPJ), familysearch.org, accessed June 14, 2022.

9. Samuel R Parkinson, Diaries, 1876–1932, Journal vol. 2, Nov. 1886– Feb. 1895, MS 1798, digitized manuscript, Church History Library, the Church of Jesus Christ of Latter-day Saints.

10. Thomas G. Alexander, *Mormonism in Transition: A History of the Latter-day Saints, 1890–1930* (Urbana: University of Illinois Press, 1986), 65–66.

11. "Arthur William Hart," FamilySearch (Person ID: KWJK-CHC), familysearch.org, accessed June 14, 2022.

12. D. Michael Quinn, "LDS Officials Involved with New Plural Marriages from September 1890 to February 1907," in *The Reed Smoot Hearings: The Investigation of a Mormon Senator and the Transformation of an American Religion*, ed. Michael Harold Paulos and Konden Smith Hansen (Logan: Utah State University Press, 2021), 278.

13. Fife American collection, 1940–1976, FOLK COLL 4, no. 1, series I, vol. 3, no. 329, Special Collections and Archives, Merrill–Cazier Library, Utah State University.

after Cowley's publication. The story was a family one for her as well, though further removed than it was for Cowley. Sandberg's grandfather was William Chandler Parkinson, the third son of Samuel and Arabella.[14] Ellen Elvira Lane Parkinson, Sandberg's grandmother, was the first of William's two wives. Even though Sandberg was born in 1910 to a monogamous household,[15] most of her polygamist grandparents and great-grandparents were alive during her childhood. Based on her detailed account below, Sandberg grew up hearing family stories about an earlier version of Mormonism that still contained polygamy and the occasional peepstone.

Hart's Story

Local Preston attorney Arthur W. Hart told his version of this story to the Fifes in 1946.[16] Hart's retelling was multilayered, as he pointed out that he didn't hear Samuel tell the story himself. Instead, a friend of Hart's heard Samuel tell the story. This structure—a story heard from a friend of a friend, but depicted as true and vouched for—is the classic indicator of a legend. A legend is a story that is potentially believable to its audience and is presented as being true.[17] Hart's version of this story strives to collapse the distance between his telling and Parkinson's by quoting Parkinson directly and articulating his thoughts.

In contrast to the Fife's version of this story, Hart made no mention of lost mules, Kaysville, or Samuel's first wife. Instead, Samuel "was going to Church down there [in Logan], and he said there was an old lady there that had a peepstone and wanted to let him take it."[18] Samuel looked into the peepstone out of curiosity and saw "two beautiful little girls coming into Church that day, all dressed in blue." Samuel then "went down there [to church] and started talking to them [the girls]. First I found out that I was to preside in Church that day. I asked the two girls if they would marry me."

---

14. "William Chandler Parkinson." FamilySearch (Person ID: KWC4-W93), accessed 14 June 2022, https://ancestors.familysearch.org.

15. "Carma Leora Smuin." Family Search (Person ID: KWC5-W29), familysearch.org, accessed June 14, 2022.

16. Fife American collection.

17. McNeill, *Folklore Rules*.

18. Brackets in original.

Hart reminisces that "In Sunday School the boys all had stories about peepstone days," suggesting that he heard this story in church. However, it is unclear from his statement whether the story was swapped casually, as gossip or storytelling for pleasure before or after Sunday school, or if it was part of a Sunday school lesson, where members may have been invited to share spiritual stories. Interestingly, this statement also seems to cement this kind of revelation firmly in the Mormon past. By 1946, the "peepstone days" could be looked back on and discussed nostalgically because that chapter of church history and culture had closed.

In Hart's story, Samuel ended his telling by focusing on his posterity. Samuel said that he had "about thirty six children, and they are all around here." Hart's humorous tone is especially clear through his choice of the word "about," which suggests even Samuel isn't certain just how many children he has. Hart had also started his story by describing it as "a little comical." The Fife's version of this story may also have been intended to be humorous, or lightly taken, as it is contextualized in a chapter called "Wise and Foolish Virgins."

Cowley's Story

Luella P. Cowley, the daughter of Samuel and his third wife, Maria Smart, contributed "The Parkinson Romance" to the second volume of *Heart Throbs of the West*, published by the Daughters of Utah Pioneers in 1940. It was published in a chapter titled "Her Wedding Journey," which contained various stories of pioneer marriages and courtships. Given the chapter and story titles, the tone of Cowley's story seems to have been romantic, or at least serious, rather than amusing.

The Fifes seem to have primarily pulled from this story, as it contains many of the same details: Samuel lost his cows in Kaysville, went to see "a man who had a peepstone," and saw the two "girls" at the suggestion of his first wife.[19] Even the structure of his wife's suggestion is the same in both stories. Cowley writes that Samuel's wife first assumed that he does have another wife ("Ask to see your other

---

19. Luella P. Cowley, "The Parkinson Romance" in *Heart Throbs of the West*, ed. Kate B. Carter (Salt Lake City: Daughters of Utah Pioneers, 1940), 14–15.

wife") and then hedged her assumption ("if there is one for you").[20] Like the Fife's version, as the couple left the peepstone scene, Samuel asked his wife, "If you ever see those two girls will you consent for me to marry them?" While in the Fife's version, she answered with a defiant challenge, "Yes ... but you'll never see them," in Cowley's story, her answer was more submissive, both to her husband and the legitimacy of the revelation: "Yes, but never until then."

Cowley's story also includes several significant details not found in the other accounts. She described significant familiarity between the Smart and Parkinson families before the second and third marriages. While the Fifes had mentioned the men opening a grist mill together, Cowley added: "Because of their business associations, they visited with each other's families." This brief sentence introduced an intimacy between these families. This intimacy is reflected again at the end of the story when Cowley described her large, polygamous family as happy and close, particularly between the children of Samuel's second and third wives. Cowley ended her narrative by describing how Samuel's second and third wives "lived in one house until there were seventeen children and when father built another house a block away and moved my mother there, it was hard to separate."

Lastly, Cowley's story emphasized Samuel's spiritual reputation and authority. While the recognition of the peepstone brides took place at church in Hart and the Fifes' stories, and Hart mentioned Samuel presiding that day, Cowley provided more detail about Samuel's church position and even placed Brigham Young at the scene. That Sunday, Cowley narrates, Brigham Young was scheduled to visit Franklin, "and elaborate preparations were being made for his visit." Samuel, as a member of the bishopric, "sat on the stand at the meeting that was held in President Young's honor." This scene carefully places Samuel in a higher position at church, both spiritually and physically; he is seated on "the stand," overlooking the congregation. Samuel is a spiritual leader in his community, and on this special Sunday, that leadership places him near the Prophet himself. From his position in the church, Samuel sees "two girls, dressed alike and walking arm in arm" enter during the opening song. Even the

---

20. Ibid., 15.

"two girls" are given a status symbol that placed them ahead of the other women in their community: "They had on new hats, the first imported hats worn in Franklin."

Parkinson's religious position in the community illustrates what folklorist Tom Mould discusses in his work on personal revelation narratives in Mormon communities. Mould shows that Mormon communities evaluate whether a personal revelation story is considered "true" largely based on the individual's spiritual reputation in that community.[21] That Parkinson holds a local leadership position in the church gives significant weight to his Mormon community's perception about the validity of his revelation. His spiritual authority is inseparable from the revelation confirmation in this version of the story.

Sandberg's Story

Carma L. Sandberg wrote the Fifes in 1972 with another version of this story. A descendent of Samuel and his first wife, Arabella, Sandberg emphasized that her version of the story came from three members of Samuel's "first family."[22] Sandberg was aware that there could be many ways this story is told; her emphasis on telling "the story first family style" implies that the other two families—Maria and Charlotte Smart's lines—may have told it with other "styles." In fact, Sandberg's story is the only story that mentions Samuel's first wife, Arabella, by name. All the stories fail to name Maria and Charlotte Smart. Sandberg even provides some insight into Arabella's thoughts, feelings, and actions in this story.

Arabella is depicted as highly moral at the beginning of the story, "remonstrating" Samuel about visiting "the Peep Stone Lady."[23] Samuel "jestingly" replied that he would bring her along with him: "You

---

21. Tom Mould, *Still, the Small Voice: Narrative, Personal Revelation, and the Mormon Folk Tradition* (Logan: Utah State University Press, 2011).

22. Fife American collection, FOLK COLL 4, no. 1, series II, vol. 18, no. 657.

23. Sandberg may well have been referring to (or conflating this character with) "the Logan Peepstone Lady," who was a well-known and frequently sought-out peepstone woman in Northern Utah. On the Logan peepstone lady, see D. Michael Quinn, *Early Mormonism and the Magic World View*, 2nd ed. (Salt Lake City: Signature Books, 1998), 252; Wayland Hand, "Magic and the Supernatural in Mormon Folklore," *Dialogue: A Journal of Mormon Thought* 16, no. 4 (Winter 1983): 59; Anthon S. Cannon, *Popular Beliefs and Superstitions from Utah* (Salt Lake City: University of Utah Press, 1984), 335; and Ian G. Barber, "Mormon Women as 'Natural' Seers: An Enduring Legacy" in *Women and Authority: Re-emerging Mormon Feminism*, ed. Maxine Hanks (Salt Lake

are good enough that nothing will hurt us." While Hart had also identified the peepstone owner as a woman, Cowley and the Fifes had gendered this character as a man "who had a peepstone." This slight grammatical difference might rhetorically imply that while the man owned a peepstone, it was not significant to his identity or role in the community, unlike the seemingly well-known Peep Stone Lady. The man "who had a peepstone" was not perceived as a "Fortune Teller" who made a living from his peepstone, as the Peep Stone Lady is described by Sandberg.

Sandberg clearly positions this Peep Stone Lady operating in Cache Valley as a social outsider, utilizing stereotypical Romani imagery through her descriptions the "Fortune Teller" living and working in a "wagon on the outskirts of town."[24] Her outsider position is also reflected in Arabella's warning to Samuel: "You know where her power comes from." The positioning of the peepstone owner as being outside of the Parkinsons' Mormon community is in sharp contrast with the old woman who simply "had a peepstone" in Hart's story. In Hart's version, the peepstone owner seemed to be part of the Mormon community and was even tied to the church scene; Samuel encountered her as he "was going to Church." Whether this woman was situated in the church or on Samuel's way to church, she is clearly considered "local" in a way the "Fortune Teller" in Sandberg's story was not.

Far from providing revelation in a religious community context, the Peep Stone Lady in Sandberg's story is paid for her services with "the proper gift of silver," and is even depicted as being greedy. After the Peep Stone Lady located his lost mules, she "told Samuel that he must listen to what she could now see in the peep stone" in hopes of getting "added compensation." After Samuel paid her again, she told him about the "two young woma [sic] dressed alike in white …

City: Signature Books, 1998), 171. My research has identified this popular peepstone woman as Elvine Petersen, a Danish immigrant who moved to Logan in 1870.

24. For example, see Mariene B. Sway, "Fortune Telling Practice among American Gypsies," *Free Inquiry in Creative Sociology* 15, no. 1 (1987): 3–6. On Romani Caravan stereotypes see Cyril Henry Ward-Jackson and Denis Edgar Harvey, *The English Gypsy Caravan: Its Origins, Builders, Technology, and Conservation* (Newton Abbot: David & Charles, 1986).

holding hands" that she saw coming out of a church meeting.[25] As they left, "both Arabella and Samuel laughed" at the Fortune Teller and her visions. Arabella doubted the vision but still informed Samuel, "when you see those two girls in white you can marry them, if and when you ever see them."

However, these choices that trivialize and otherize the peepstone woman's role in the community seem to clash with the second half of the story, when Sandberg casts the vision as spiritual revelation and emphasizes Samuel and Arabella's religious, economic, and social obligations to enter plural marriage. While the scene depicting the peepstone woman's vision took place in a very liminal space—in a wagon on the outskirts of town—the confirmation of the vision happens on the stable and patriarchal church steps. This shift in scene is also reflected in a tonal shift: while Samuel and Arabella had mistrusted and laughed at the Peep Stone Lady, an outsider who was not an integrated part of their religious and cultural community at the beginning of the story, once the revelation is properly situated in the Church setting, it is taken seriously by the Samuel, Arabella, and the storyteller.

Sandberg provides some insight about Arabella's reaction after she and Samuel saw the "Smart sisters, in white, coming down the steps ... in front of the Church." Sandberg writes that "Arabella was overwhelmed by the coincidents [sic]."[26] Then Sandberg offers a long sentence detailing Arabella's thinking after this scene: "Though Arabella had known for some time that polygamy was in the offing, for all leaders in the Church, at that time, she had hoped that it would not come to her but having given her word, she lived by it, and the religion for which she had come thousands of miles acrossed [sic] ocean and prairie and mountain, leaving relatives and loved ones in England."[27]

It is significant that this is all one sentence, grammatically forcing an intimate connection between each of the sentence's points. The ideas connected are tiered: first, Arabella's knowledge that polygamy was expected for church leaders; second, her own hesitation; third,

25. Brackets original.
26. Brackets original.
27. Brackets original.

the significance of living by "her word"; and fourth, her religion as intimately connected to her history of suffering. Rhetorically, Sandberg's sentence insists that these ideas must all be held together, even if the connections between each part of this sentence may not be completely clear. This is in sharp contrast to the one-word insights the Fife and Cowley stories provided about Arabella's reaction. In the Fife's story, Arabella "confessed" to Samuel that the girls at church "look exactly like the girls we saw in the peepstone," and Cowley writes that Arabella "reluctantly" confirmed the vision.

In contrast to Arabella's complex sentence outlining her knowledge, resistance, and ultimate acceptance of polygamy, Samuel immediately "realized that he, too, must obey all of the Lord's commandments" and marry the two young women. His response incorporated social and economics motivations: "There was a limit on the marriage opportunities for the young women within the confines of religious faith and Mormon population. Samuel was prospering and could afford to keep more than one family. It was his duty to live his religion." Samuel argued that he ought to enter polygamy out of duty to his community and his religion—which were, of course, the same thing. His response sandwiched these practical social and economic justifications for marrying the young women between strong and religious language. By the end of the story, Arabella and Samuel saw his fated marriage to the two young women as a "duty" they would "live by."

Sandberg ended her story on the staggering number of descendants that came from Samuel marrying Maria and Charlotte Smart: "From these two sisters there was an issue of 24 children making Samuel's family a large patriarchal one. Today the descendants of this man are over 7,000." The implication of this conclusion is that the revelation was true and that the marriages were right because of their theological and progenic success. The Parkinson family literally grew church membership, but they also mirrored the eternal goals of Mormon men and women: to parent many spirit children.[28] Cowley's story ended on Parkinson's children from his second and third marriage as well but focused on their shared housing and tight

---

28. Johnathan A. Stapley, *The Power of Godliness: Mormon Liturgy and Cosmology* (New York: Oxford University Press, 2018).

bond; in Sandberg's story, the descendants of Parkinson and his three wives are depicted as a massive network of "over 7,000" souls. Sandberg's emphasis on this large number illustrates the tremendous impact Samuel's second and third marriages had on his legacy and descendants.

Conclusion

Cowley was a teenager when one anonymous critic described the persistent popularity of peepstones in the *Deseret News* in 1885. The critic described how peepstones were "found in the hands of men, women, and children," and used for a variety of purposes. Individuals looked to see "lost animals or stolen goods, the character of a man or woman with home the enquirer is anticipating marriage … the sex, also the future of an unborn child."[29] As the church became increasingly centralized and hierarchical towards the twentieth century, the more charismatic revelation practices, such as peepstones, became increasingly disjointed from mainstream religious practice. As anthropologist Ian G. Barber writes, "This cautious approach to charisma [in Utah] apparently hardened by the turn of the century."[30] Bruce R. McConkie explicitly denounced the practice in his 1958 book, *Mormon Doctrine*: "In imitation of the true order of heaven whereby seers receive revelations from God through a Urim and Thummim, the devil gives his own revelations to some of his followers through *peep stones* or *crystal balls*."[31] By Cowley's death in 1962, peepstones and polygamy had grown increasingly distanced from Mormon cultural identity and memory.

When Sandberg wrote to the Fifes in 1972, the Peep Stone Lady in her version of the story had become a caricature of a social outsider. Sandberg went to great lengths to distance the Fortune Teller and her peepstone from her ancestor's Mormon community. Sandberg's version of the story created a clear separation between the Peep Stone Lady working "on the outskirts of town" and her ancestors' divine revelation confirmation scene on the steps of the church.

29. "Astrology and Kindred Topics. Evils That Should Be Avoided by the People," *Deseret News*, Mar. 18, 1885, 143.
30. Barber, "Mormon Women as 'Natural' Seers," 173.
31. Bruce R. McConkie, *Mormon Doctrine* (Salt Lake City: Bookcraft, 1958), 566. Emphasis original.

While polygamy had perhaps been familiar or comprehensible to Sandberg, who knew and likely spent time with polygamous grandparents and great-grandparents in her youth, by the second half of the twentieth century, peepstones had been pushed far outside of Mormon personal revelation narratives.

When D. Michael Quinn's *Early Mormonism and the Magical World View* was published in 1987, the ground-breaking and densely researched book drew widespread attention in the field of Mormon studies. In the introduction, Quinn wrote, "my re-examination of early Mormonism from this new perspective provides an interpretative tool for weaving together what otherwise appear as loose threads of the Mormon past." By reexamining the more magical early elements, such as treasure digging, diving rods, peepstones, amulets, and astrology, and rejecting "the boundaries of officially approved [Mormon] history," Quinn contextualized many of the (previously felt to be) "loose threads" in early Mormon history. Quinn acknowledges that "not all of these threads are of equal weight, strength, or value."[32] Yet, as a folklorist, I would argue that closer examinations of many of these small threads will provide new insights on Mormon culture and history.

The story of the peepstone brides may well be one of these small threads. It was never widely known or widely circulated in the larger Mormon community. Before Cowley published her version of "The Parkinson Romance" in 1940, it seems the story was maintained orally. It was passed on as a family story and a local one. But by listening closely to these storytellers in their historical contexts, this story begins to reflect Mormon culture's shifting attitudes about the more magical roots of Mormonism from 1940 to 1972 and the enduring interest and effects of polygamy on the progeny who descended through it.

---

32. Quinn, *Early Mormonism*, xxi.

The Gentle Curse of Dreams: Eugene England and the Biopolitics of Latter-day Saint History

CALVIN BURKE

He looked like Robert Redford and was just as charismatic.[1]

Unlike Redford, however, the young professor was insistently Mormon. He kept his hair cut short and his clothes relatively conservative in style. He was also brilliant. He held graduate degrees from MIT and Stanford, and possessed a knowledge of the Mormon past, its history, and its theology deeper than almost any of his era. Then, on September 12, 1979, little more than two years into his career at Brigham Young University, the young professor took the stage at BYU's Varsity Theater to speak about God and education to a group of honors students. Though initially well-received, the young professor's remarks sparked a brutal, public confrontation with one of the highest doctrinal authorities in all of Mormonism: Apostle Bruce R. McConkie.

The young professor's name was Eugene England, later christened a founder of Mormon studies.[2] The public "war" between England and McConkie, one of the most influential apostles of the

---

1. This essay a critical counter-mythopoetics of Latter-day Saint history. It is an attempt to retell the foundational metanarratives of Mormon historiography from a perspective that emphasizes the embodied experience of marginalized adherents. This is not intended as an accusatory exercise, merely a reading that bathes the same facts of Mormon history in the light of a different perspective. This essay draws heavily upon postsecular theory, queer theory, and performance studies, perhaps most notably the following works: See, for instance: Foucault, Michel, Michel Senellart, François Ewald, and Alessandro Fontana, *Security, Territory, Population: Lectures at the Collège de France, 1977–1978* (New York: Picador/Palgrave Macmillan, 2009); Judith Butler, *Excitable Speech: A Politics of the Performative* (New York: Routledge, 1997). Giorgio Agamben, *Homo Sacer: Sovereign Power and Bare Life* (Stanford: Stanford University Press, 1998); Peter Coviello, *Make Yourselves Gods: Mormons and the Unfinished Business of American Secularism* (Chicago: University of Chicago Press, 2019).

2. Terryl L. Givens, *Stretching the Heavens: Eugene England and the Crisis of Modern Mormonism* (Chapel Hill: University of North Carolina Press, 2021).

twentieth century, that ensued following England's 1979 address, largely defines public conception of both men in popular imagination. At dispute was the concept of God's eternal nature—does he continue to progress and learn, or has he always been omniscient? In response to England's remarks, McConkie delivered multiple public addresses denouncing England's ideas as "deadly heresies," and an ostensibly private letter to England that threatened both his eternal and professional damnation was circulated worldwide.

In spite of the scale of retribution, the disagreement between England and McConkie has largely been treated as a squabble over a minor tenet of Mormon theological esoterica made unnecessarily public by McConkie's personal pride and eagerness to assert his position as a doctrinal authority. The story of Eugene England's life is therefore taught as a tragic, cautionary tale about "ark-steadying" within Mormonism.[3]

And yet this narrative leaves much unexamined. Why did one of the most influential apostles in twentieth-century Mormonism—an international church by then consisting of millions—consider the remarks of an untenured English professor given to a few dozen undergraduate students worthy of denunciation not once, not twice, but thrice, in international, church-wide fora? What was it about a speech, the thesis of which was upheld by generations of prominent Mormon leaders past, that sent one of the most powerful men in Mormon leadership to DEFCON-1? In short, what was so threatening to Bruce R. McConkie about Eugene England?

To answer this question, we first must attempt to define what Mormonism is, and what the chief concerns of the Latter-day Saint faith are.

Mormonism, like many western religions, is socially constructed. Yet Mormonism is not characterized by a coherent set of unchanging beliefs or a systematic theological system. Indeed, as James Faulconer has argued, Mormonism is an "atheological" religion.[4] Kristine Haglund has elsewhere ruminated that the practice of

---

3. See Givens, *Stretching*, 160–82.

4. James E. Faulconer, "Why a Mormon Won't Drink Coffee but Might Have a Coke: The Atheological Character of the Church of Jesus Christ of Latter-day Saints," in *Faith, Philosophy, Scripture* (Provo, UT: Neal A. Maxwell Institute for Religious Scholarship, 2010), 87–107.

defining Mormon theology is akin to "nailing Jell-O to a wall."[5] However, it must be argued that twentieth-century Mormonism's philosophical incoherence is a feature, and not a bug.

Mormonism is not concerned with being coherent. Mormonism is instead concerned with producing coherence. By "producing coherence," I mean producing bodies that perform. Bodies that obey. Bodies that look and act and talk and think and behave in the world in a very certain way. This is a feature, not a bug.

By this I mean that Mormonism is performative. To paraphrase Kathleen Flake and Lowell Bennion, Mormonism is not something one thinks or believes. Mormonism is something one does.[6] Mormonism is not a way of thinking or believing or hoping, or at least, not only; Mormonism is an embodied way of being and living and acting in the world. And Mormon thought is kept brilliantly by its people, incoherent and abstract, so that it may also be malleable to fit whatever command they may require of themselves or those around them. To be philosophically incoherent is to be extraordinarily useful.

Mormonism is defined by its concern for all that really exists of itself in the world. Which is to say that Mormonism is defined by its concern for its tangible objects, its buildings—chapels, temples, universities—as well as by what it requires of the performances of those who occupy its buildings.

By this I mean that Mormonism is a biopolitics.[7] Which is to say that Mormonism is deeply concerned with regulating the performances of those who occupy its buildings. It cares deeply enough to

---

5. Kristine Haglund, "Finding the Mormon Voice," remarks originally delivered at Claremont Graduate University in 2010, in possession of the author. It will be important to also note that Haglund determines that—if placed within a container such as a cup—it may be possible, in fact, to nail Jell-O to a wall. For particularly sophisticated attempts at nailing the aforementioned Jell-O to a wall, in addition to Haglund's body of work, see Sterling McMurrin, *The Theological Foundations of the Mormon Religion* (Salt Lake City, UT: The University of Utah Press, 1965).

6. Kathleen Flake, "The LDS Intellectual Tradition: A Study on Three Lives" (Salt Lake City: The Obert and Grace A. Tanner Humanities Center at the University of Utah, 2014). Flake's comments came during the Q&A portion of the Spring 2014 Sterling M. McMurrin Lecture on Religion and Culture, available at YouTube.com, at the 56 minute mark: "[In regard to] the particular system that is Mormonism, I think you have to do Mormonism to get it. And I think if you don't do it and just think about it, as an intellectual, I'd say, you don't get it from that great of a distance."

7. See Peter Coviello, *Make Yourselves Gods: Mormons and the Unfinished Business of American Secularism* (Chicago: University of Chicago Press, 2019).

regulate the way that Mormons behave. Its leaders conduct regular audits of all adherents, beginning at age eight. Compliance is recorded at its lowest levels and delivered to its highest levels. Those who fall short of performing proper Mormonism are encouraged to correct their performances. Those who do not correct their performances cease to be in good standing with Mormonism. Those who transgress continually are forbidden from performing Mormonism entirely. This, too, is a feature, and not a bug.

Mormonism is a hierarchy of bodies.[8] Mormonism values certain kinds of bodies more than other bodies. Under the dictates of contemporary Mormonism, only certain types of bodies can perfectly perform Mormonism. Other types of bodies are not allowed to perform Mormonism. Only the perfectly performing Mormon bodies can make decisions about other kinds of Mormon bodies. The bodies that Mormonism values most are those it allows to have the power to make decisions about other bodies. Poor bodies, queer bodies, female bodies, disabled bodies, and racialized bodies are often not valued as much as other bodies in our twentieth-century Mormonism.[9] These bodies are often not granted means to perform Mormonism perfectly. Mormonism does not believe these bodies can ever perform Mormonism sufficiently for them to have power, much less to define Mormonism for other bodies. If these bodies were to be given power, Mormonism would cease to be Mormonism. Or rather, Mormonism would be a different kind of Mormonism than what contemporary Mormonism has become. And Mormonism cares very deeply about the kind of Mormonism that it is. This, too, is a feature, not a bug.

Mormonism was not always performed in the way that contemporary Mormonism is. In the past, to be a Mormon meant being and doing things that were profoundly at odds with what the rest of the world, especially America, considered good, and proper, and right. America has always been deeply concerned with what it considers

8. See Isabel Wilkerson, *Caste: The Origins of our Discontents* (New York: Penguin Random House, 2020).

9. See Taylor Petrey, *Tabernacles of Clay: Sexuality and Gender in Modern Mormonism* (Chapel Hill: University of North Carolina Press, 2020). See also W. Paul Reeve, *Religion of a Different Color: Race and the Mormon Struggle for Whiteness* (New York: Oxford University Press, 2015).

good, and proper, and right behavior. Mormonism has also always been deeply concerned about the way that Mormon bodies perform, and has constructed regulatory systems to shape the way that Mormon bodies behave. Our current performance of Mormonism, and the regulatory structures that encourage the particular way of being Mormon they encourage began to take shape at the end of Mormonism's transition beyond polygamy, in the early twentieth century.

Mormons from the very beginning were in tension with the Americans. In one of those rare, messianic moments in time, as the people who would experience it would attest, the divine, the transcendent, the "all-surpassing and all-confusing" reached down, touched ground, and animated the bodies of some people who before had performed as good Americans.[10]

These bodies—these god-touched bodies—became the first Mormons. These first Mormons and their bodies did not perform in the world like the Americans believed that Good Americans should behave. And for this, the Americans chased the Mormons from place to place. The Americans persecuted the Mormons. After the Mormons tried for some time to defend the Mormon way of being as an alternative yet good way for an American to be, they failed to impress the Americans. The Mormons decided they would rather be Mormons than Americans. They fled the country rather than continue trying to be Americans.

And yet, the Americans found them again. And the Americans still did not believe the Mormons could be both Mormons and Good Americans. The Americans felt they could not live peacefully with Mormons behaving the way Mormons behaved. And the Mormons insisted that to be Mormon meant to be and to do what they were doing. And so began a very long struggle, at times even a war, where the Mormons sought to redefine what it meant to be Good Americans, and the Americans, in turn, sought to stop the Mormons from behaving like Good Mormons. And so went the battle.

After this struggle, a war of many years, the Mormons failed to

10. Both in stylistic rejection of—and deeper solidarity with—the trappings of postsecular theory, I use the terms "American" and "secular" as roughly interchangeable—for if we consider the definition of "secular" proposed by Coviello in *Make Yourselves Gods*, as "the racialized theodicy of hegemonic liberalism"—is it still possible to distinguish "the American" from "the secular"?

redefine what it meant to be a Good American. The Mormons, instead, changed what it meant to be a Good Mormon. From that moment on, in the eyes of the Americans, the Mormons became Good Americans. And so the war ceased.[11] Yet in the eyes of many older Mormons, the Mormons ceased to be Mormons. Or rather, the Mormons became a different kind of Mormons, a kind of Mormon the older Mormons had never thought possible.

Then a new generation was born. For the first time, these children found themselves at once Mormons and Americans at birth. These Mormon children found opportunities in America that their ancestors never dreamed of. Prospects, acceptance, and power were dangled before their eyes. But they were haunted. Everywhere in this newfound world, they were haunted by the memories of their ancestors. They were mocked for their ancestors. These new American Mormons were not trusted because of their closeness, their similarity to their un-American ancestors. So these Mormon children looked back upon the bodies of their ancestors from a new perspective, the perspective of Americans.

These children of the Mormons looked at the un-American performances of their ancestors, and they were ashamed. Mormon men had sex with many different women. Worse, these Mormon men married the women they were having sex with, for the whole world to know. They canonized this deviant, un-American sex in their scriptures as a requirement for salvation. The Mormons had been sexual deviants! This could never be allowed to happen again.

These American children of the Mormons—these Mormons torn between being Mormon and American—they looked again upon the bodies of their ancestors and saw them sacralizing Indigenous people. Even worse, this sacralization of the Indigenous was canonized, repeatedly, in their scriptures. Even though this White Savior narrative was simply another form of colonialism, these American Mormons saw their Mormon ancestors as race-traitors. This could never be allowed to happen again.

These Mormon children who wanted to be Americans looked upon

---

11. I am indebted to both Michel Foucault and the evocative counterhistory of nineteenth-century Mormonism provided by Coviello in *Make Yourselves Gods*, which provide much of the reading of the history within these paragraphs.

the bodies of their ancestors a third time, and beheld they were abolishing private property. The Mormons encouraged women to work outside the home, to be educated. Worse, their church financed the educations of women, and encouraged their activism in support of their rights. The Mormons looked quite a bit like communist radicals. Worst of all, these practices—which looked quite a bit like socialism—were canonized in their scriptures. The American children of the Mormons saw their parents were anticapitalist traitors! And gender traitors, to boot! This could never be allowed to happen again.

In short, the children of the Mormons found themselves torn between being Mormons and being Americans. And they wanted to be Americans more than they wanted to be Mormons. So they created systems, systems a lot like the American systems, systems designed to produce bodies of Mormons that would perform an American kind of Mormonism. And they changed what it meant to be Mormon, and buried the memories that testified otherwise. They wanted it to become impossible for anyone—any Mormon or any American—to ever remember a time when Mormons were not Good Americans.

The Mormons, then, became American, and they grew in favor and in standing with the Americans and the world they governed. And then America began to rule the world, and the Mormons were anxious to be ruled and to rule alongside them. And so the American children of the Mormons soon forgot they had ever been anything but American. And the years passed, in relative peace.

But then something happened. Something that happens everywhere and always and often in the world and in America. Somewhere, something transcendent reached down, touched ground, and animated the bodies of people who previously had performed as good Americans.

We begin the scene: The 1960s. The Bay Area of California. It was the dawning of the Age of Aquarius, and not even the Mormons would sleep through it.[12] The wildfire at Berkeley was kindled in equal terms by politics and the FBI,[13] but at Stanford, the Farm

12. James Rado, Jerome Ragni, and Galt McDermot, "Aquarius," from *Hair: The American Tribal Love-Rock Musical* (New York: 1967).
13. Seth Rosenfeld, *Subversives: The FBI's War on Student Radicals and Reagan's Rise to Power* (New York: Picador, 2013).

across the bay, a little slower to wrath, slower to kindle, the fires were sparked not by J. Edgar Hoover's ineptitude and paranoia, but by something far worse, something far more radical—perhaps the most dangerous thing a nation-state like America could ever face:

Someone was teaching Jesus at Stanford University.

Three people—theologians, no less—were teaching Jesus at Stanford. And they were teaching Jesus, not teaching *about* Jesus. Though Stanford's charter forbade the university from allowing the three theologians to evangelize, the gentlemen elected instead to teach modern theology and ethics. They were teaching not what Jesus did, but what Jesus would do. Which is to say, they were teaching Christianity that followed Jesus to the end of Jesus' teachings. They were teaching Applied Christianity. The most dangerous kind of Christianity. And the students were responding. Their religion courses quickly became some of the most popular elective courses on campus, with over seven hundred students registering for a single section one year. This absurdity, this total disregard for propriety was happening at a good, American, secular, rigidly nonsectarian, private university, a university which less than fifteen years earlier had been derided by the total lack of attention to religious affairs which its campus community paid—and, importantly, would not even have a full faculty or formal department of religion until 1973.[14]

But the Sixties were what historians would declare "The Golden Decade of Religious Studies" at Stanford University.[15] Theirs was an era characterized by unprecedented religious popularity, and what one astonished Stanford Professor in 1969 declared "an explosion in the objective study of religion unmatched in the history of American education."[16] The student body was caught up and animated in a fervor of religion that national media outlets declared "one of Stanford's most adventurous intellectual disciplines." This "Renaissance of Religion," as *Time Magazine* christened it in 1966, began four years earlier in 1962 with the appointment of the ringleader theologian, a man named Robert McAfee Brown, who, while the board of

14. Van Harvey, "Religious Studies at Stanford: An Historical Sketch," *Sandstone and Tile* 22, nos. 2 and 3 (Spring/Summer 1998): 3–10. The "someones" teaching religion were B. Davie Napier, Michael Novak, and Robert McAfee Brown.

15. Harvey, "Stanford," 6.

16. William Clebsch, "Religious Studies Soar," *Stanford Daily*, Jan. 10, 1969, 4.

trustees formally voted to hire him, was languishing in a jail cell in the American South for leading a Civil Rights march.[17]

When the students at Stanford were pollinated on the Farm by the same fervor that hit Berkeley across the bay, it should be no surprise that the theologians, the most popular professors on campus, became their greatest defenders. The theologians gave them religious justification for their protests—the theologians were standing on the barricades beside them, pleading their causes before administration in religious terms, and defending the students to the broader public. Women's liberation, Civil Rights, gay liberation, it was all at Stanford in the Sixties. And religion and the radical, un-American teachings of these theologians were at the heart of it, not the only the voices but the leading voices—on the barricades, in the marches, at the sit-ins. Religion gave the students the practical tools and the ethical justification for their opposition to everyday realities in America. To be American, they taught, did not always mean to be good.

This was the Stanford of the Sixties where young Mormon institute instructor Eugene England found himself.[18] And England, ostensibly at Stanford studying with the legendary Wallace Stegner, mentor of American luminaries from Wendell Berry to Sandra Day O'Connor, fell under the spell of McAfee Brown and become his teaching assistant.[19] And England, the young Mormon graduate student, was transfixed and transformed.

And so, when Eugene England took the stage at BYU more than ten years later in 1979 to speak about God and education, he was simply applying what he had learned at graduate school. And England taught Jesus, sure, but he also taught other dangerous things, like Joseph Smith. His legendary address, though it has never been released to the public, has been represented in popular imagination as simply a meditation on God as an eternal student. This is incorrect.

17. "Theology: Faith and Learning at Stanford," *Time,* Nov. 25, 1966; Harvey, "Stanford," 6.

18. Eugene England, "Finding Myself in the Sixties," ca. 1993, unpublished manuscript, Eugene England Papers, box 50, fd. 4, ACCN 2426, Special Collections, J. Willard Marriott Library, University of Utah.

19. Eugene England, "Becoming a World Religion: Blacks, the Poor—All of Us," *Dialogue: A Journal of Mormon Thought* 27, no. 4 (Winter 1998): 52–54. See Givens, "Stretching the Heavens," 278: "[Gene] was profoundly influenced by both the theology and iconoclastic role played... by his mentor, Robert McAfee Brown of the Reformed tradition."

For though England discussed at length the then-newly resurrected King Follett discourse, the idea of a God who learned to be
God, he followed Joseph Smith's teachings to their logical conclusion. Perhaps most startlingly, England's address used the teachings
of Joseph Smith to answer the question posed by its title, which was
"The Lord's University?" (complete with a question mark).[20]

For the titular question, "Is BYU the Lord's University?," the
answer England determined and guided his audience to was, "No,
BYU is not." But how did England get there?

England began with an old Mormon couplet: "As Man is, god
once was; as God is, man may be." Joseph Smith taught the fall of
Adam and Eve was a good thing, England said, because only with
free agency could the children of God become like God. When we
forget that God's own journey to godhood involved learning and
growing, England explained, we also forget that we are called to
learn and to grow. Life, as Joseph Smith explained, was a positive
universe of adventure. But at BYU, England beheld a university
body in chains, where the administration regulated not merely class
offerings and the styles of hair and articles of clothing that could
cover their bodies, but even the questions the students could ask and
study in their religion courses.

At BYU, students were not allowed to question. They were forced
to be good. They were machines at BYU, not Gods in embryo. England argued that this plan of coercion over conversion was "*exactly
the Devil's plan*" (emphasis in original). BYU was in flagrant vio-
lation of the restored teachings of Joseph Smith. BYU could not
therefore be properly described as "The Lord's University," or—
both beautifully and terrifyingly—not yet. England then implored
the students of BYU to cast off from their minds "the gloom, the
depressing shadow" of traditional, American, "apostate concepts of
God and pessimism about the earthly condition of man."

England called upon the hymnal words of Parley Pratt:

The Morning Breaks, the Shadows Flee,
Lo, Zion's standard is unfurled.

---

20. Eugene England, "The Lord's University?," unpublished essay, 1979, England
Papers, box 54 fd. 5.

The dawning of a brighter day,
Majestic gathers on the world.

England then concluded, "Let us return to the God of Abraham, of Isaac, and Jacob. The God of Joseph, of Brigham, and Lorenzo."

England was opening Pandora's box. He was invoking a return to an un-American Mormonism—a performance of Mormonism that held an equal and compelling and conflicting claim upon the bodies of the Mormons. England's speech was nothing short of a direct dismantling on the myriad of biopolitical engines—what Althusser termed "ideological state apparatuses"[21]—developed by Mormon leaders to encourage a performance of Mormonism that created bodies fit for the powers of the same American empire that Joseph Smith and the early Mormon contemporaries denounced. McConkie's overwhelming response, seen from this perspective, makes far more sense. The threat posed was not personal, but existential. Heaven forbid that BYU students get the same ideas as the students in Berkeley, to say nothing of Nauvoo.

But to focus on McConkie and the Mormons is to miss the forest for the trees. The Mormons were merely using the tools afforded them. Consider, too, the tools utilized at Stanford to bring the radicals to heel. Stanford, like all secular American universities, was and is a machine designed to produce good American bodies. When Stanford found itself producing radicals who believed they could and should change the world, Stanford used different methods. Rather than yield to the calls of God and its student protestors, Stanford responded by forming a formal religious studies department and ensuring the theologians were removed from its faculty. Stanford, where unsecular religion had been both believed and applied, soon became a place where religion was only to be studied, not taught. Robert McAfee Brown, the first and the last of the three musketeering theologians who had tutored England, resigned from Stanford in 1975. The un-American became American once more.[22]

But lest it be forgot, 'twas in the Sixties, this golden era of Stanford, this place of forgotten and most peculiar religious fervor, this burned

---

21. See Louis Althusser, "Ideology and Ideological State Apparatuses" in *Lenin and Philosophy and Other Essays*, trans. Ben Brewster (London: New Left Books, 1971).

22. Harvey, "Stanford," 8–10.

over district, which inspired its students not to believe in Jesus, but to believe Jesus. This Jesus taught its students, like Joseph Smith did, that "to be American" did not mean "to be good." This Jesus caused its students to become leaders in the Civil Rights and the Black Panthers and psychedelic and anti-war movements, to found both the Esalen Institute and *Dialogue: A Journal of Mormon Thought*.[23]

The roots of Mormon studies are in this radical, un-American, unsecular activism. It should be no surprise then that during a time when Mormonism was intent on performing as wholly American, wholly secular, that un-American, unsecular bodies gravitated towards *Dialogue* and Mormon Studies. In that time of concerted, embodied forgetting, a new subsection of un-American Mormons took shape. And with their un-American performing bodies, they unburied and resurrected the un-American bodies of their ancestors. They staked their claim to belonging within an American Mormonism by demonstrating that the "traditionally American" Mormon body then being encouraged by the American children of the Mormons was not so traditional at all.[24] It was here in the Sixties at Stanford and beyond that some Mormons, like their unsecular, unamerican ancestors, each developed, to quote the poet Ocean Vuong, "a skull thick enough to keep / the gentle curse of dreams."[25]

Eugene England was by no means the only Mormon intellectual afflicted with the gentle curse of un-American dreams. Present just at the same campus where England taught his un-American Mormonism were other leading lights of the New Mormon History: Jill Mulvay Derr, Richard Bushman, Scott Abbott, David Knowlton, and Cecelia Knochar Farr. Each of these people produced history and work that differed from the "state-sanctioned real," as determined by Salt Lake City.

One intellectual with a thick-skull and dreams was historian D. Michael Quinn, also present at BYU chronicling Mormonism's forgotten past. Born queer, Chicano, and Mormon, Quinn's magisterial

---

23. Jeffrey J. Kripal, *Esalen: America and the Religion of No Religion* (Chicago: University of Chicago Press, 2007).

24. See, for instance, Maxine Hanks, ed., *Women and Authority: Re-Emerging Mormon Feminism* (Salt Lake City, UT: Signature Books, 1992).

25. Ocean Vuong, "Essay on Craft," Poetry Foundation, July/August 2017, poetry-foundation.org.

exposition of Mormon archival material was compelled by a relentless faith in his religion and an earnest fidelity to Mormonism's history. As Quinn wrote thousands of pages resurrecting some of the most controversial elements of Mormonism's past, he provided consistent evidence demonstrating the inherent claim that marginalized bodies such as his held to a place within the Mormon covenant. Though neither his work nor his queer, Latine body were acceptable to his contemporary church leaders, the groundbreaking historiography Quinn recovered in an era of forgetting is what makes possible the existence of modern Mormon studies, including critical reconsiderations of the Mormon past like this one. Mormon studies owes its very existence to bodies like England's and Quinn's—non-normative bodies haunted by dreams of Mormonisms otherwise, bodies they consecrated to the restoration of a Mormonism that offered differing—even liberatory—visions of human destiny.

Dreams such as these cause no small unpleasantness, both within and without Mormonism. It should be no surprise then that, like the authorities at Stanford and elsewhere, the American children of the Mormons responded in kind—at Brigham Young University and beyond, and both Quinn, England, Farr, and many other intellectuals, found deep pain at Brigham Young University and within their faith.

In a time when to be American meant to be powerful and capitalistic and racist and homophobic and transphobic and imperialistic and misogynistic—it should come as no surprise that the Mormons, after a struggle of their own, chose to be American. It should be no surprise that the American children of the Mormons were stricken with shame once again at the thought of being perceived like the hippie radicals, the queers, the feminists, the communists—each more than a little like what their ancestors had been.[26] Most Mormons wanted to be American more than they wanted to be Mormon. And they received their reward. But others—those cast aside, down, or out—those with thick skulls, kept the gentle curse of their dreams. They, too, received their reward—and it shall not be taken from them.[27]

26. See, for example, Ernest L. Wilkinson, "Make Honor Your Standard," address given at Brigham Young University, Sep. 23, 1965, copy in author's possession.

27. See, for instance, McKay Coppins, "The Most American Religion," *The Atlantic*, Dec. 16, 2020. "Perpetual outsiders, Mormons spent 200 years assimilating to a certain national ideal—only to find their country in an identity crisis."

And so, for a time, things grew quiet once more. And the Mormons grew in favor and in standing with the Americans and the world they governed. And the American children of the Mormons forgot once again that they had ever been anything but American. But then, something happened, something which happens everywhere and always and often in the world and in America:

What it meant to be a good American began to change.

The Perils of Social Change and Strategic Meltdowns at the Mormon Flagship University, 2007–2021

BRIANNA BRATSMAN

On August 23, 2021, Brigham Young University invited its faculty and staff to participate in a university conference to kick off the fall semester. President Kevin J. Worthen opened the meeting by announcing a new Office of Belonging designed to "root out racism" and "combat prejudice of any kind." He concluded his address by quoting President Spencer W. Kimball, the twelfth president of BYU's sponsoring institution, the Church of Jesus Christ of Latter-day Saints (LDS Church). Because most Latter-day Saints remembered Kimball for lifting the LDS Church's racial restrictions on priesthood ordination and temple ordinances in 1978, his quote offered special significance in the context of diversity and inclusion. "We expect—we do not merely hope—that Brigham Young University will become a leader among the great universities of the world," Kimball had pronounced in 1976. However, he added a caution: BYU must also "remain a unique university in all the world!"[1]

1. Acknowledgements: the author would like to thank Dr. Rebecca de Schweinitz, the research supervisor, for her patient guidance, enthusiastic encouragement, and useful critiques of this research work. Additionally, the author would like to thank Dr. Ben Park, Makoto Hunter, Kaitlyn Hillam, Michael Bratsman, Dayne Bratsman, and Erin Bratsman for their insight that greatly assisted the research, as well as comments that substantially improved the manuscript.
    Kevin J Worthen, "An Obligation to the World," speech given Aug. 23, 2021, at the 2021 University Conference of Brigham Young University, speeches.byu.edu; On Kimball and the racial restrictions, see Edward L. Kimball, "Spencer W. Kimball and the Revelation on Priesthood" *BYU Studies* 47, no. 2 (2008): 4–87. From 1852–1978, the church prohibited Black members of African descent from receiving ordination to its priesthood offices (normally granted to all adult men members in good standing) or worshiping in its temples, the church's most sacred spaces (normally accessible to all adult men and women members in good standing). The church ended the policy when

Worthen's remarks and echoing of Kimball's historic position were in line with other recent actions by the university to address issues of inclusivity. Six months earlier, BYU released a sixty-three-page report that identified "the sources and effects of racism at BYU" and included twenty-six specific recommendations, including the creation of an Office of Diversity and Belonging.[2] Shortly before that, members of the university had expressed hope that the report would lead to "real changes that make BYU a better, more inclusive place for all."[3]

Immediately following President Worthen's remarks, which seemed to signal that the university was committed to becoming more inclusive, LDS Apostle Jeffrey R. Holland addressed the crowd. Holland's speech struck a different tone. Referencing letters he had received from distressed members of the church, Elder Holland lamented how "some people in the extended community are feeling abandoned and betrayed by BYU. It seems that some professors," Holland continued, "are supporting ideas that many of us feel are contradictory to gospel principles, making it appear to be about like any other university our sons and daughters could have attended. Several parents have said they no longer want to send their children here or donate to the school." Seeming to accept the validity of the accusations, Holland expressed unease about reports that identified BYU programs and professors as "radicalizing" attitudes and "destroying" faith.[4]

Elder Holland's rhetoric only grew more aggressive from there. He quoted the late apostle Neal A. Maxwell, who had warned that scholars at BYU must work with a "trowel in one hand and a musket in the other," because "scholars building the temple of learning must also pause on occasion to defend the kingdom." The "trowel" and

---

it announced a revelation in 1978, during Kimball's presidency. Church members in the United States widely celebrated the end of the restrictive policy, and the "revelation on priesthood" came to define Kimball's legacy.

2. Shane Reese et al., *Report and Recommendations of the BYU Committee on Race, Equity, and Belonging* (Provo, UT: Brigham Young University, February 2021).

3. Ben Frandsen (@benfrandsen), "Very grateful for the good work done by the @ BYU Committee on Race, Equity, and Belonging over the past year," Twitter, Feb. 26, 2021, 12:46 p.m., twitter.com. Frandsen is an assistant professor at BYU.

4. Jeffrey R. Holland, "The Second Half of the Second Century of Brigham Young University," speech, Aug. 23, 2021, Brigham Young University, speeches.byu.edu.

"musket" metaphor came from a long Mormon tale of how Saints had to stand watch for mobs while building the Nauvoo Temple. Holland did not leave the intended direction of these muskets ambiguous. After a brief assurance that he and others in the church's highest leadership were aware of the complicated feelings surrounding marriage and the "same-sex topic" on campus, the apostle expressed indignation that a recent graduate had "commandeered a graduation podium ... to announce his personal sexual orientation." This was a direct criticism of former student Matty Easton for his April 2019 commencement speech in which he used that opportunity to publicly declare that he was gay—a statement that was widely understood to have been approved by the university administrators.[5] Finally, Holland chastised the BYU community for its "recent flag-waving and parade-holding"—likely referencing BYU's first Pride and other protests—because such activities were not in line with prophetic leadership and revealed doctrine.[6]

Students and other members of the Mormon community flocked to social media to share their disappointment, hurt, anger, and disgust. To them, Elder Holland's speech appeared to be the antithesis of the spirit of inclusion and belonging described by President Worthen. The disparity was so striking it appeared intentional—a message that BYU would only go so far in its quest to increase belonging. During Worthen's talk, Addison Jenkins, former president of the school's largest LGBTQ+ group and unofficial club, USGA, tweeted, "Cautiously optimistic that this will lead to *real* *tangible* *observable* changes that make Brigham Young University a safer place for the thousands of PoC and LGBTQ students that study there each year."[7] Two hours later, he tweeted, "I'm taking this back *unequivocally* based on this talk that Elder Holland gave from the same pulpit minutes after Worthen."[8] Calling Worthen's talk a "bait

5. Matty Easton, "What I've Learned since Coming Out in My BYU Commencement Speech Last Year," *Good Morning America*, June 22, 2020, goodmorningamerica.com.

6. Holland, "The Second Half."

7. Addison Jenkins (@AddisonDJenkins), Twitter, Aug. 23, 2021, 10:06 a.m., twitter.com.

8. Addison Jenkins (@AddisonDJenkins), Twitter, Aug. 23, 2021, 12:35 p.m., twitter.com.

and switch," Jenkins's observations of the contrast between the two addresses were shared by many in the university community.[9]

But while the attitude of Worthen's talk juxtaposed with Holland's fiery address was disappointing, it seemed familiar. Over the last decade and a half, significant changes around LGBTQ+ issues have occurred at BYU, but these changes have also been accompanied by anti-LGBTQ+ rhetoric and policies. This essay explores how discussions about equality and inclusion at BYU on the part of administration, faculty, and students have developed in uneven and unexpected ways at the LDS Church's flagship university.[10]

There is a long context that brought BYU to this moment. Taylor Petrey and other scholars have theorized and documented the circuitous route that resulted in LDS teachings on sexuality and gender. Significantly, Petrey suggests the importance of BYU's role in the LDS Church's relationship with social issues. While other scholars have studied the way BYU's infamous aversion therapy program both influenced and was influenced by church rhetoric at the time, Petrey asks further questions about the relationship. Moreover, he identifies important parallels between the church's approach to race and LGBTQ issues.[11] Similarly, scholars who have studied the role that BYU has played in the LDS Church's racial history have shown the significance of national perceptions of BYU's racism as well as the importance of BYU faculty and administrators in perpetuating racial mythology. Their work shows the importance of and provides a model for looking at how social issues play out at BYU. In both contexts, gender and race, BYU has played a large role in how the LDS Church has managed its image and message.[12]

---

9. Addison Jenkins (@AddisonDJenkins), "STOP LIKING THIS TWEET I TAKE IT BACK IT WAS A BAIT AND SWITCH," Twitter, Aug. 23, 2021, 3:51 p.m., twitter.com.

10. Throughout the paper, the words "queer" and "LGBTQ+" will be used interchangeably. Although the most inclusive term is typically agreed to be "LGBTQIA+," I have chosen to use "LGBTQ+" instead because discussions about intersexuality and asexuality have only recently been included in wider queer discussions, and they have historically not been a part of the conversations around queer issues at BYU.

11. Taylor G. Petrey, *Tabernacles of Clay: Sexuality and Gender in Modern Mormonism* (Chapel Hill: University of North Carolina Press, 2020).

12. Madison Harris, "'The Hands of Our Enemies': Brigham Young University and the Federal Government in the Fight for Civil Rights, 1968–1975," (senior thesis, University of Colorado, 2020), 86–109; Rebecca de Schweinitz, "'There Is No Equality': William E. Berrett, BYU, and Healing the Wounds of Racism in the Latter-day Saint

My research centers on BYU's relationship with LGBTQ+ issues from 2007–2021. A variety of sources—including official BYU sources, faculty publications, social media posts, and interviews with BYU community members—demonstrate recurring conflicts within and between the BYU community and the LDS Church. For this essay, I will be focusing on the related, yet distinct actions taken by administration, faculty, and students. These patterns reflect the ways that BYU has historically dealt with issues of race, and these parallels are crucial to understanding the process of social change within the university, and the LDS Church.[13]

D. Michael Quinn would have been familiar with these tensions, even if he did not live long enough to witness Holland's address. As a closeted gay man while employed as a BYU professor, he knew well what it meant to hide his true identity to fit institutional policies; and as someone who was forced to resign from his position, he was well aware of what it was like to push back against administration. This was the world that shaped Quinn, his fellow professors, as well as the school's thousands of students.

Administration

BYU's administration is heavily resistant to social change. In the last fifteen years, those who have held these positions have almost never responded to calls from its students for queer inclusion and acceptance, only changing course when its discriminatory policies make national news. In October 2016, for example, the Big 12 decided not to admit BYU as a member of its athletic conference after significant backlash about BYU's "homophobic, biphobic and transphobic policies and practices."[14] That same month, BYU

Past and Present," *Dialogue: A Journal of Mormon Thought* 52, no. 3 (Fall 2019); Matthew L. Harris and Newell G. Bringhurst, eds., *The Mormon Church and Blacks: A Documentary History* (Urbana: University of Illinois Press, 2015); Darron T. Smith, *When Race, Religion, and Sport Collide: Black Athletes at BYU and Beyond* (Lanham, MA: Rowman & Littlefield, 2016).

13. Because of the breadth of the topic, I could not include the specific and unique experience and treatment of BYU trans and non-binary students, but their experiences should be studied further. Additionally, I have not addressed the intersectionality of race and sexuality in this paper, but I hope to further explore the experiences of queer students of color in the future.

14. "25 LGBT Groups Send Letter to Big 12 Urging It to Shun BYU," *Fox Sports*, Nov. 15, 2016, foxsports.com.

administrators "sought out an invitation" to Common Ground, an NCAA forum to "explore how LGBTQ and faith-based communities can work more cohesively in college sports and higher education," and the university hosted the forum two years later.[15] BYU also put together a "working group" of faculty, staff, students, and experts to discuss ideas on how to increase inclusion for queer students.[16] The Big 12 reversed its decision in 2021 and officially invited BYU to the conference, and many suggested that the university's work with Common Ground and the working group was instrumental to the decision.[17]

However, while the university was rewarded for its progress, queer students saw little tangible change. The working group members, for instance, were barred from creating an on-campus club for queer students.[18] BYU removed the section from its honor code that prohibited homosexual behavior but later clarified that no policies had actually changed. When facing national pressure, therefore, the administration enacts performative policy changes that rarely alleviate any actual problems that marginalized students face at the university. This has been BYU's rule of thumb for decades. When it faced accusations of racial discrimination in the 1960s, BYU enacted what Rebecca de Schweinitz calls a "disingenuous approach to Black student admissions." Worried that outright prohibiting Black applicants from attending BYU would "be far more detrimental to [BYU] and the church than the danger of a chance intermarriage," BYU Vice President William Berrett and other leaders established a series of precautions the university could take to limit Black attendance while still appearing to have a non-discriminatory admissions process.[19] For decades, then, BYU has responded to national criticisms by implementing gilded social policies without palpable substance.

15. Rachel Stark, "An Uncommon Conversation," *NCAA*, Nov. 21, 2017, ncaa.org; Natalie Tripp Ipson, "Finding Common Ground," *Y Magazine*, Winter 2019, magazine.byu.edu.

16. Rachel Stark-Mason, "Breaking Ground," *NCAA*, Jan. 22, 2019, ncaa.org.

17. Jay Drew, "The Story behind This Associate AD and Her Contribution to BYU's Big 12 Invite," *Deseret News*, Sep. 9, 2021, deseret.com.

18. Stark-Mason, "Breaking Ground."

19. de Schweinitz, "There Is No Equality," 67–68.

Community Responses

In addition to national pressure, BYU receives a lot of feedback, especially on social issues, from the broader Mormon community. For most universities, their larger circle consists mainly of those on campus, alumni, and locals. However, because of BYU's unique position as a church university, many people with any connection to the LDS Church—whether they be active members, ex-Mormons, or others who inhabit the Mormon cultural region—are deeply invested in BYU's policies and decisions. Thus, when BYU—or any of its faculty, staff, or administration—makes decisions oppositional to popular community views, the university is bombarded with messages demanding change.

In my interviews, I spoke with administrators, faculty members, and students who had all been the target of calling campaigns at the university. There are numerous examples of them receiving community pressure, but I will highlight one. Renata Forste, the international vice president at BYU, told of her experience hosting the first university-sanctioned panel on homosexuality in 2012. As the Sociology Department Chair, she had approved the panel for a small, sociology-department-only event. Somehow, flyers advertising the event were posted in the Wilkinson Student Center. Outrage immediately followed. University administration, the Dean, and Dr. Forste all received threatening and hateful phone calls, emails, voice messages, and letters demanding that the event be canceled.[20]

Latter-day Saints with conservative politics have long been expressing their displeasure with decisions or individuals at the university. Richard Poll, a history professor at BYU from 1948–70, was the subject of many concerned letters to BYU President Ernest Wilkinson. In a letter reminiscent of the one Holland read in his recent address, one man wrote about Poll, "Many of our Church members are happy that they can send their children to B.Y.U. so that they won't be indoctrinated by liberal thinkers who make it a special point to discredit anti-communists and their publications."[21] When

---

20. Renata Forste, interview with the author, Nov. 4, 2021.
21. Gary James Bergera, "The Richard D. Poll and J. Kenneth Davies Cases: Politics and Religion at BYU during the Wilkinson Years," *Dialogue: A Journal of Mormon Thought* 45, no. 1 (Spring 2012): 51.

Poll invited Dorothy Marshall to speak about civil rights to a small group of graduate students in 1963, Latter-day Saints criticized the decision, expressing concerns about Marshall's past affiliation with civil rights groups. Critics published letters in local papers to alert the community.[22] Afterward, Wilkinson told Poll that there was "little chance for his further advancement" at the university.[23]

Poll's critics were not exclusively found in lower levels of church membership, however. Apostle Ezra Taft Benson also spoke to President Wilkinson to suggest that BYU needed a "real house-cleaning" to get rid of Poll and other professors. Poll also clashed with several other leaders, including then-president of the Quorum of the Twelve Apostles, Joseph Fielding Smith. The push was eventually successful. Although he was a "popular and effective teacher,"[24] Poll knew that his critics in the community and church leadership had ensured that he would not advance any further in his career at the university and that his days at BYU might be numbered. So, he resigned to accept a position at another university in 1969.

Faculty

Poll's story is not unique. He is one of numerous faculty members who have been fired or pushed out of BYU due to their activism, making the fear of retaliation a real and present danger.[25] In my interviews with faculty, every single one of them brought up their concerns about getting fired. Several requested that I keep their comments anonymous. This dynamic is crucial in understanding faculty's role in social movements at the university. These fears come from BYU's sometimes contradicting positions as an institution of faith and an institution of scholarship and learning. Professors are supposed to hold up the doctrine and principles of their faith while also publishing research that meets a disciplinary standard.

For example, Erin Holmes, the director of the School of Family Life, explained that professors in her department are expected to

22. Eugene Bryce, letter to the editor, *Daily Universe*, Apr. 21, 1965.
23. Bergera, "Richard D. Poll," 43–73.
24. Ibid., 52.
25. I would be remiss if I did not point out the similarities between Poll's experiences as a BYU faculty member with those of Mike Quinn, the man whose legacy this publication is meant to honor.

produce two kinds of publications: academic work that fits with the university standards, and what is called "public scholarship"—works that inform local and national audiences on family life, which includes "engaging constructively" on matters of core importance to BYU and the church.[26] The 2020 Public Scholarship Report contains works published in the *New York Times*, the *Institute for Family Studies*, the *Ensign*, the *Deseret News*, and other public venues.[27] BYU faculty are therefore put in a unique position where they are expected to meet academic standards with their research and instruction while simultaneously upholding the church's position on LGBTQ+ issues.

One of the many results of these stipulations is a growing split within faculty beliefs.

Many professors and administrators discussed this split with me, but it was most apparent when walking past faculty offices. The halls of the Joseph F. Smith building (which hosts the humanities and social sciences) are filled with pride flags displayed outside many office doors, something not found in many of the other buildings at BYU. Professors gave two main reasons for the discrepancy. First, professors in the humanities and social sciences often have to confront these issues in their academic studies. As university professors, they are expected to contribute credible research to their fields—fields which are often examining the experiences of LGBTQ+ people.[28] Second, they talked about the impact of their interactions with students that identify as LGBTQ+. A meta-analysis of queer students in American higher education found that almost 40% of queer-spectrum students were arts, humanities, or social sciences majors.[29] So professors in these departments directly interact with more students who identify as LGBTQ+, meaning they will hear directly from queer students about their experiences and challenges.[30]

However, the split within faculty beliefs is not cleanly divided along department lines. Not all office doors in the Joseph F. Smith

26. Erin Holmes, interview with the author, Nov. 4, 2021.

27. Hal Boyd and Kaylin Cash, *Public Scholarship Report* (Provo, UT: BYU School of Family Life, Aug. 31, 2020).

28. Anonymous, interview with the author, Nov. 22, 2021.

29. Maren Greathouse et al., *Queer-Spectrum and Trans-Spectrum Student Experiences in American Higher Education: The Analyses of National Survey Findings* (Rutgers Tyler Clementi Center, August 2018), 33–34.

30. Anonymous, interview with the author, Dec. 7, 2021.

Building display pride flags. One professor explained that his colleagues put up the church's Family Proclamation outside their offices
to signal that they do not agree with LGBTQ+ "agenda," as well as
to show disdain for the ally professors.[31] The same dividing lines that
are causing contention among the church writ large are present in
BYU departments, albeit at a smaller level.

Students

Finally, I examined the role of student voices in BYU's relationship with LGBTQ+ issues. Scholars have mostly found a lack of
student push for change on issues of race at BYU during the 1960s
and 1970s. Unlike other universities at the time, BYU held no protests on campus about civil rights.[32] However, student protests and
demonstrations at BYU about LGBTQ+ issues have regularly occurred since at least 2019.

Why are students so much more involved now than they were
before? For one, the issue is more personal. A 2020 study found
that 13.2% of BYU students identify as something besides "strictly
heterosexual."[33] Conversely, only two Black students attended BYU
in 1965.[34] Even currently, a half-century later, less than 1 percent of
undergraduates at BYU are Black. Grace Soelberg, a recent graduate
from BYU, explained that people "can't turn off [their] Blackness,"
but LGBTQ+ students generally have the choice to hide their queerness.[35] Queer students have therefore been able to covertly attend
BYU in a way that Black students could not: for the most part, they
can choose who knows about their marginalized identity. Thus, BYU
has never been able to effectively limit queer attendance like it has
Black attendance.[36] Since researchers have found that relationships

31. Anonymous, interview, Nov. 22, 2021.
32. Gary James Bergera, "Student Political Activism at Brigham Young University,
1965–71," *Utah Historical Quarterly* 81, no. 1, (Winter 2013): 65–90.
33. Jared S. Klundt et al., "Sexual Minorities, Mental Health, and Religiosity at a Religiously Conservative University," *Personality and Individual Differences* 171, (Mar. 2021).
34. Grace Ann Soelberg, "Peculiar Students of a Peculiar Institution: A Historical
Analysis of Racial Minority Students and Race Relations at Brigham Young University
as Presented in the Banyan From 1911–1985," (undergraduate honors thesis, Brigham
Young University, 2021).
35. Grace Soelberg, interview with the author, Nov. 2, 2021.
36. For BYU limiting Black attendance, see deSchweinitz, "There Is No Equality,"
67–68.

with LGBTQ+ people are "associated with decreased homophobia," the presence of queer students at BYU directly influences campus attitudes toward LGBTQ+ issues.[37]

In addition to having more exposure to the queer community on campus, BYU students are much more connected to the outside world than they were fifty years ago. At the time of the *Brown v. Board* Supreme Court decision, only one-fifth of the student population read a newspaper other than the BYU-published *Daily Universe*.[38] During this time, Wilkinson heavily censored the *Daily Universe* and forbade several topics like "Negro and the priesthood and other racial problems."[39] Because news and opinions were filtered almost exclusively through campus sources, students were unlikely to form conclusions contrary to university or church policies. Now, the internet gives students access to news and opinions from all over the world with no interference from BYU or the church.

Countless social media platforms provide a place for students and other community members to make friends, spread information, and create support networks. At the time of writing, Instagram accounts @usgabyu, @loveisneverwrongbyu, @usga.so, @theoutfoundation, @cougarpridecenter, @colorthecampus, and @raynbow.collective—a non-exhaustive list of accounts dedicated to the queer community at BYU—had a combined 24.8k followers. On Twitter, the keywords "BYU" and "gay" return 36.9k results. The chat platform Discord hosts a server called "BYULGBTQ" where students can connect with their queer peers in channels such as "general-conference," "safe-space," "church-discussion," "media-discussion," and even "memes."[40]

Social media has also been used to share information about BYU policies and its treatment of queer students. In early 2020, BYU removed the clause about homosexuality from its honor code, only

37. Barbara Finlay and Carol S. Walther, "The Relation of Religious Affiliation, Service Attendance, and Other Factors to Homophobic Attitudes among University Students," *Review of Religious Research* 44, no. 4 (June 2003): 370. When studying homophobic attitudes among university students, researchers found that "the number and type of relationships to known lesbian, gay, or bisexual others influences attitudes strongly: more relationships and closer contact are associated with decreased homophobia."
38. "We Go Pogo," *Daily Universe*, Sep. 22, 1955.
39. Bergera, "Student Political Activism," 87.
40. @Czarcasm2jjb, interview with the author, Nov. 4, 2021.

keeping the section that forbade all students from "sexual relations outside a marriage between a man and a woman." This news quickly spread through social media, with multiple Twitter users reporting their conversations with the Honor Code Office confirming that students in homosexual relationships would be held to the same standards as those in heterosexual relationships.[41] News organizations like the *Washington Post* quickly picked up the story and used social media posts from students as a main source of information. In their article, the *Washington Post* referenced six different social media accounts.[42]

However, two weeks later, BYU released a letter "clarifying" that same-sex romantic behavior was still against the honor code. The BYU community then demonstrated how social media can also be used to broadcast their hurt, anger, and disgust.[43] Calvin Burke—a prominent queer Mormon and the most followed BYU student on Twitter in the months leading up to the honor code change—explained, "I had learned to master the art of the strategic meltdown, which is like: you're queer, you're at BYU. You're going to be breaking down crying all the time. So you can do that in your shower, or you can do it in the office of the Dean of Students and make someone else see it and experience your trauma vicariously with you."[44] BYU's tweet announcing the clarification received over 1,000 replies and almost 2,000 quote tweets, forcing BYU to reckon with a public display of the anguish this flip-flop caused its community members.[45] BYU students use social media to have strategic meltdowns that render the negative effect of queerphobic policies visible

41. Tad Walch, "Church Updates Honor Code for BYU, Other Schools," *Deseret News*, Mar. 4, 2020, deseret.com; Emma (@emmalee0326), "Hey just wanted to let people know that we called the HCO and the official words were "living a chaste and virtuous life means as long as you don't have sexual," Twitter, Feb. 19, 2020, 1:01 p.m., twitter.com; @fremlo, "It is confirmed. Gay dating is okay, kissing and hand holding from the mouth of an HCO counselor. Featuring my first gay kiss @Kate_Foster14," Twitter, Feb. 19, 2020, 2:12 p.m., twitter.com.

42. Marisa Iati, "BYU Removed Its Longtime Ban on 'Homosexual Behavior,' but Many Students Still Have Questions," *Washington Post*, Feb. 21, 2020, washingtonpost.com.

43. Tad Walch, "New Letter Clarifies Update to BYU's Honor Code Following Weeks of Confusion," *Deseret News*, Mar. 4, 2020, deseret.com.

44. Calvin Burke, interview with the author, Nov. 17, 2021.

45. BYU (@BYU), "Today This Letter from Elder Paul V. Johnson, Commissioner of the Church Educational System, Regarding the Updated Honor Code Was Sent to Students and Employees," Twitter, Mar. 4, 2020, 11:14 a.m., twitter.com.

to otherwise distant administrators and to broader publics capable of enacting consequences: holding the university accountable in ways that would otherwise be impossible, as students are grossly disadvantaged within the power dynamic at the university.

Conclusion

Social change within the Church of Jesus Christ of Latter-day Saints cannot be fully understood without looking at the part BYU plays. Battles about LGBTQ+ issues are being fought at BYU, and the church's racial history suggests that the outcomes directly influence church policy and teachings. The debates about equality and inclusion that have taken and continue to take place at the LDS Church's flagship university embody the broader tensions taking place in Mormonism more generally.

D. Michael Quinn experienced these tensions during the interregnum between the civil rights debates and the LGBTQ+ movement. As a queer man himself, Quinn was compelled to closet his own homosexuality to remain in good standing as a church member, a BYU professor, and an aspiring apostle. Quinn's publications disobeying church censorship and contradicting church narratives consistently landed him in hot water with administration, culminating in his forced exit from BYU. Moreover, Quinn's excommunication from the church five years after his departure from BYU indicates that issues at the heart of debates, advocacy, and retaliation at BYU mirror the issues at the heart of tensions within the LDS Church.

D. Michael Quinn, A Postscript

MARTHA BRADLEY EVANS

Many of us who attended the D. Michael Quinn symposium in May 2022 were reminded of the value of a single life. Michael's life mattered. It mattered to those of us who were his friends or his colleagues, it mattered to those who read his history or heard him talk, it mattered to the course of Mormon historiography.

As a person. I remember most Michael's voice. His resonant tones reached into the lower ranges which always had a sort of question in it like he was probing us for a better understanding or better argument. It was most often coupled with a kind smile, a slight tilt downward of his head, or a belly laugh as he threw his head back and let his amusement take over his body. Michael was a good friend who never missed sending Christmas cards regardless of where I moved, who never missed a birthday or a chance for a connection. But then there were terrible gaps when he sort of disappeared for a time in Mexico or in California, trying to carve out new lives.

His life stages. His life had distinct stages—the challenges of his youth, his time as a young father, husband, and scholar. His time as a beloved and inspiring faculty member at Brigham Young University, and then his time afterwards as he chased fellowships, teaching gigs, grants, and publications. Much of his last years was solitary, searching for connection, maintaining long term friendships, but mostly alone.

His vulnerability. Michael's vulnerability was striking. I understand that he was not always easy to edit and battled sometimes with those who worked with him to polish his manuscripts. A certain intellectual arrogance underpinned this resistance to change that made him sometimes a difficult collaborator. There was a compelling vulnerability about him, not quite humility but an eagerness to be accepted, to be valued, to be respected, always searching to be seen.

I suspect Michael felt deeply misunderstood, that the pain of the public scrutiny of his motivation and his person cut to his core. His excommunication always seemed like a tremendous mistake.

His sense of calling. I remember multiple times being with Michael in sessions at Sunstone, at MHA, and hearing him talk about his belief in visions, his sense of calling, and a belief that his life was meaningful in a way he didn't quite understand but also that he felt chosen. Many times in his lifetime his leaders—both ecclesiastical and professional—told him as much and he held onto the idea in a sort of love/hate relationship with Mormonism that was never resolved. Painful to observe, I remember wishing that he didn't care so much so it wouldn't hurt in the way it did.

His pathbreaking. D. Michael Quinn's scholarship is legendary and made an outstanding contribution to Mormon History. He finally received the Leonard J. Arrington Award from the Mormon History Association for his lifetime of contributing to the history of the Church of Jesus Christ of Latter-day Saints in 2016. He was a tireless researcher, known for his exactitude, mining primary sources with unparalleled energy, meticulousness, and care. When he was on a project, he was frequently in the Church History Library, running through sources, taking careful notes, and engaging with colleagues and friends in the reading room. His footnotes are the stuff of legend reflecting the complexity and thoroughness of his mind, his process, the sources he had consulted, or those that others should as well. His footnotes guide scholars of all stages to ask other questions or do further research, following where the sources lead.

Michael was a pathbreaker who wrote landmark articles or chapters in books that changed the course of future study. The book that really put Michael on the map was *Early Mormonism and the Magic World View*, a work that distanced Mormon history from its alleged supernatural origins to a more secular or cultural world view that saw magic as a reasonable explanation for those elements that were difficult to comprehend. His article "LDS Church Authority and New Plural Marriages, 1890–1904," on post manifesto polygamy, set the standard for all studies that would come afterwards and demonstrated the extent of plural marriages that proceeded after the Manifesto of 1890 supposedly concluding the official practice of a plurality of wives. Particularly important was his tracking of key LDS leaders who continued in the practice themselves or persisted in performing plural marriages in the decades after the Manifesto. This created, in part, the confusion that led to the origins of the Mormon Fundamentalist movement. His *Dialogue* article on homosexuality and the Mormon Church, "Male-Male Intimacy among Nineteenth Century Mormons, a Case Study," probed the surface pronouncement of heteronormativity, and suggested a quite different reality beyond view and laid the ground work for his later volume, *Same-Sex Dynamics among Nineteenth-Century Americans.*

His series of volumes on Mormon hierarchy give a sweeping view of the human beings who built Mormonism and their political, economic, social, and religious lives. *Mormon Hierarchy*, again, lays out most of the issues others would take up in their own work, exhibiting a thoroughness that reveals the key source materials, analyzes their usefulness, and forms a critique of the motivation, inspiration, and development of the organizational structure of the LDS Church. Somehow saying these three volumes (and his book about LDS Leadership and finances) are pathbreaking doesn't quite capture how important they are. They lay out the framework and pathway in an incredibly complex, intricate, and intriguing way that is both engaging and a little overwhelming, and ultimately helps us look at the Mormon past in a profoundly different way.

Our loss. Even for those of us who cared about Michael, and I am one of them, Michael was an enigma. In all his brilliance, his exemplary work ethic and intellectual purity, he was so profoundly human, so flawed. He was a friend, colleague, and exemplar who opened his heart wide open and asked us to truly see him and to care and respect him. Many of us did. He is already missed.

About the Authors

Ian Barber teaches archaeology and anthropology at the University of Otago, New Zealand, where an indulgent if sometimes bemused employer supports his periodic research and occasional teaching in Mormon studies. Ian has also pursued Mormon studies research and teaching with a focus on race, culture change, and uses of the past as a Fulbright New Zealand Scholar in anthropology at Brigham Young University in 2011, and as Marlin K. Jensen Scholar and Artist in Residence at the Tanner Humanities Center, University of Utah, between 2018 and 2019.

Gary James Bergera was the director of publishing at Signature Books from late 1984 to 2000, then the managing director of the Smith-Pettit Foundation from 2001 to 2022 (both headquartered in Salt Lake City). He is author/co-author or editor/co-editor of several books, including the diaries of Leonard J. Arrington, published in three volumes as *Confessions of a Mormon Historian*. His one-volume annotated abridgement of the diaries of Ernest L. Wilkinson, president of Brigham Young University during the 1950s and 1960s, is forthcoming. His publications have received awards from the Charles Redd Center for Western Studies, the Dialogue Foundation, the John Whitmer Historical Association, the Mormon History Association, and the Utah Historical Society. He served on the editorial boards of the *Journal of Mormon History* and the *John Whitmer Historical Association Journal* from 2014 to 2022. He received the Leonard J. Arrington lifetime achievement award from the Mormon History Association in 2018.

Martha Bradley Evans has taught at the University of Utah for almost thirty years, where she has also held a number of administrative positions. She has won prestigious awards for both her teaching and scholarship, including the Mormon History Association's Leonard J. Arrington Award for Distinguished Service. Her many books include *Kidnapped from that Land: The Government Raids on the Short Creek Polygamists, Pedestals and Podiums: Utah Women, Religious Authority, and Equal Rights,* and *Glorious in Persecution: Joseph Smith, American Prophet, 1839–1844.*

Brianna Bratsman is a graduate of Brigham Young University in Provo, where she researched race, gender, and rights. Her interest in these topics stemmed from her involvement in queer groups on campus, including USGA and BYU LGBTQ. She also participated in many demonstrations and protests throughout her time at BYU, including multiple Rainbow Days and honor code protests. She hopes to continue her study of history as an independent researcher and eventually at the graduate level.

Calvin Burke has served as research assistant to Drs. Anthony Sweat, James Faulconer, and Terryl L. Givens of the BYU Neal A. Maxwell Institute, and as a media manager for *Dialogue: A Journal of Mormon Thought.* Deeply involved in advocacy efforts at the intersection of queer rights and Mormonism, Burke has been a featured guest on NBC News and NPR, and his advocacy efforts have been featured in many outlets, including *Xtra Magazine, Salt Lake Tribune, Daily Beast,* the *Independent, Chronicle of Higher Education,* and *Washington Post.* In 2022, in recognition for his advocacy efforts, The Center for American Progress in Washington, DC, selected Burke as one of their "Faith Leaders to Watch."

Maxine Hanks is a historian and theologian of gender in religion, specializing in Mormon studies and Christian liturgy. She earned her bachelor's in gender studies at the University of Utah, and her master's work in history at ASU, with graduate theological studies at Harvard as a ministry fellow. She lectured in women's studies at the University of Utah for ten years and has guest lectured at many schools. She edited *Women & Authority: Re-emerging Mormon Feminism,* published by Signature Books in 1992. She was excommunicated from the LDS Church along with collaborator Michael Quinn as one of the September Six in 1993, then later rebaptized in 2012, and has since held a number of callings or positions within the LDS Church.

Hovan Lawton graduated from Brigham Young University with a bachelor's degree in history, a secondary degree in Spanish studies, and a minor in Latin American studies. He is currently in a master's program in history at Utah State University. His research interests include nineteenth-century Latter-day Saint history in the US West, as well as the history and development of the Church of Jesus Christ of Latter-day Saints in Latin America.

Patrick Mason is a professor of religious studies and history at Utah State University, where he holds the Leonard J. Arrington Chair of Mormon History and Culture. He is the author or editor of several books about Latter-day Saint history, theology, and culture, most recently *Proclaim Peace: The Restoration's Answer to an Age of Conflict*, co-authored with David Pulsipher.

K. Mohrman is a clinical teaching track associate professor of Ethnic Studies and serves as affiliated faculty in the Women and Gender Studies and Religious Studies programs at the University of Colorado Denver. Her first book, *Exceptionally Queer: Mormon Peculiarity and U.S. Nationalism* was published with the University of Minnesota Press in 2022. Her work has also appeared in venues such as *Radical History Review*, *Mormon Studies Review*, *Journal of International and Intercultural Communication*, *American Religion*, and *Routledge History of American Sexuality*, among others. She is the recipient of the 2018–2019 LGBTQ Religious History Award.

Benjamin E. Park received his doctorate in history from the University of Cambridge and is an associate professor of history at Sam Houston State University. He is the co-editor of *Mormon Studies Review*, editor of *A Companion to American Religious History* (Wiley-Blackwell), and author of *Kingdom of Nauvoo: The Rise and Fall of a Religious Empire on the American Frontier* (Norton/Liveright), which won the Mormon History Association's Best Book Award. He is currently completing a general survey of Mormonism in America for W.W. Norton's Liveright imprint.

Sara M. Patterson is a professor of Theological Studies and Gender Studies at Hanover College. Her works include *Middle of Nowhere:*

Religion, Art, and Pop Culture at Salvation Mountain (University of New Mexico Press) and *Pioneers in the Attic: Place and Memory Along the Mormon Trail* (Oxford University Press). She is currently working on a book about the September Six, intellectuals who were disciplined by the LDS Church in 1993.

Cristina Rosetti is an assistant professor of humanities at Utah Tech University. Her research focuses on the history of Mormon fundamentalism in the Intermountain West. Her first book, a biography of Saint Joseph White Musser, is forthcoming from University of Illinois Press. She is currently editing Musser's journals and correspondences with Bryan Buchanan for publication.

Millie Tullis is a poet and folklorist from northern Utah. She holds an MFA in poetry from George Mason University and is currently studying folklore at Utah State University. In 2022, she won the Annaley Naegle Redd Student Award in Women's History from Charles Redd Center for Western Studies, the Best Unpublished Graduate Student Paper Award from the Mormon History Association, and the Elaine J. Lawless Graduate Student Travel Award sponsored by the Folk Belief and Religious Folklife Section of the American Folklore Society. She is the editor-in-chief of *Psaltery & Lyre*, an online journal publishing literature at the intersection of faith and doubt.

Sujey Vega is a daughter of Latinx immigrant parents. She is the director of the Community Engaged Initiatives program, an associate professor of Women and Gender Studies and affiliate faculty member in the School of Transborder Studies and Religious Studies at Arizona State University. Her book, *Latino Heartland: Of Borders and Belonging in the Midwest* (NYU Press, 2015), places in dialogue ethno-religious practices, comadrazgo (female social networks), Whiteness, and Mexican ethnic solidarity in a Midwestern city. Vega's current project locates the growth of Latina/o LDS members and the role the LDS Church plays in the lives of Latina/o Saints. She has several publications out on Latina/o Saints and is finishing a forthcoming book on the subject. Additionally, as a director of the Community Engaged Initiatives program at ASU, Vega is training students to redefine research relationships and prioritize community members themselves as leaders on projects.

Neil J. Young is a historian, writer, and podcaster in Los Angeles, California. He is the author of *We Gather Together: The Religious Right and the Problem of Interfaith Politics* (Oxford, 2015). He is currently working on a book about the history of LGBTQ Republicans for the University of Chicago Press. Young's scholarly works have appeared in the *American Quarterly*, the *Journal of Policy History*, and several edited volumes. He writes frequently about religion, culture, and American politics for publications like the *New York Times*, *Washington Post*, *Atlantic*, *Slate*, *Los Angeles Times*, *Vox*, and *Politico*. Young co-hosts and produces the popular history podcast, *Past Present*. He holds an AB from Duke University and a PhD in US history from Columbia University. He previously taught at Princeton University.